Columbia University

Contributions to Education

Teachers College Series

No. 262

AMS PRESS
NEW YORK

THE FUNCTIONS OF COURTS IN ENFORCING SCHOOL ATTENDANCE LAWS

BY

JOHN FREDERICK BENDER, Ph.D.

PROFESSOR OF SCHOOL ADMINISTRATION
UNIVERSITY OF OKLAHOMA

Teachers College, Columbia University
Contributions to Education, No. 262

Bureau of Publications
Teachers College, Columbia University
NEW YORK CITY
1927

Library of Congress Cataloging in Publication Data

Bender, John Frederick, 1879-
The functions of courts in enforcing school attendance laws.

Reprint of the 1927 ed., issued in series: Teachers College, Columbia University. Contributions to education no. 262.
Originally presented as the author's thesis, Columbia.
Bibliography: p.
1. Educational law and legislation--United States --States. 2. Education, Compulsory--United States-- States. I. Title. II. Series: Columbia University. Teachers College. Contributions to education, no. 262.

KF4158.Z95B4 1972 344'.73'0792 79-176550
ISBN 0-404-55262-5

Reprinted by Special Arrangement with Teachers College Press, New York, New York

From the edition of 1927, New York
First AMS edition published in 1972
Manufactured in the United States

AMS PRESS, INC.
NEW YORK, N. Y. 10003

ACKNOWLEDGMENTS

In the task of collecting, organizing, and interpreting the data for this study the author has had the very generous assistance of many people. Officials in state departments of education, in attendance departments in city schools, and in courts for the enforcement of attendance laws have freely given indispensable help. They have made available the necessary records and have verified the items of fact on which the study is based. To all these officials the author is most grateful.

He is under special obligations to Dr. Carter Alexander, Dr. Frederick G. Bonser, and Dr. Harry D. Kitson, of his dissertation committee, Teachers College, Columbia University, for their advice in determining the limits of the study, and for a critical reading of it after it was completed. Dr. Alexander served as chairman of the above-named committee, and gave continuous and effective guidance over a period of many months. Especial thanks are due him for his consistent efforts to make this undertaking a success.

J. F. B.

TABLE OF CONTENTS

THE FUNCTIONS OF COURTS IN ENFORCING SCHOOL ATTENDANCE LAWS

CHAPTER I

INTRODUCTION

A constant problem in school administration is the improvement of attendance on instruction. School boards endeavor to assist by providing attractive sites and buildings and adequate equipment. Superintendents, supervisors, and teachers offer solutions by improving the organization, course of study, and methods of presentation. A specialized attendance service has been developing in the better-organized systems with trained workers whose task is to discover and remove the causes of nonattendance. To improve the quality of this service has been the purpose of some recent careful studies.

As an adjunct to better attendance, school systems are providing a health service which aims at keeping children in school more days in the year and in a condition to profit most by the school experience. As a further aid to attendance, some legislatures have provided that books and supplies shall be furnished free. Some have provided, too, for cases of economic need by legalizing assistance in the form of mothers' pensions, scholarships, school lunches, and aids for indigence, all with the view of making regular and profitable attendance on instruction possible.

State legislatures have enacted laws compelling attendance of children of specified ages for a specified period of time each year. The legislatures also define the limits within which exemptions to the requirements of attendance are legal. Not only have legislatures passed laws compelling attendance, but they are constantly modifying and amending these laws so as to add more years of required attendance for each child and longer periods of attendance each year.

Complementary to legislation requiring school attendance is the legislation restricting child labor. This legislation is aimed not only at protecting children from the hazards of harmful occupations, but at safeguarding their time as well so that attendance at school may take place under conditions most favorable for learning. In addition, an elaborate system of taxation has developed which brings in vast sums of money yearly to support a scheme of free public education. The theory of this system is that every person, whether he has children or not, shall be taxed according to his means for the purpose of making free public education possible. This theory of taxation was once limited to the local school district, but now it is being applied to larger units like townships, counties, and states on the principle that wealth wherever it may be found shall be required to contribute to the education of children wherever they may be found. The extension of this principle to the entire nation has many and very powerful advocates.

Taxation for free public education is compulsory. No one legally escapes its requirements. If the man with means must contribute of his means to furnish education to the children of other men, it seems reasonable that the man with children shall be compelled—if compulsion be necessary—to have his children regularly at the appointed place of instruction thus furnished. In addition to all the agencies that are provided to make school attendance possible for those who are eager to take advantage of it, society is providing agencies to compel the attendance of those who seek to escape it. That there are those who do seek to escape it needs no proof. Exact information on the proportion who seek to escape is not easy to obtain. In one investigation, it was found that in one state the number of persons convicted for violation of the compulsory attendance law in 1914 was 722; in 1920, it was 2,462. The percentage of convictions of persons arrested was 12.85 in 1910 and 33.37 in 1921.[1]

Among other things, these figures suggest that some persons must be compelled to cause attendance of their children at

[1] Hanson, W. L. *The Costs of Compulsory Attendance Service in the State of New York*, pp. 32 and 37.

school, and that one of the agencies of compulsion is the courts. Taking these as basic facts, this study endeavors—

A. To assemble data on methods and degree of enforcement of attendance laws by courts and other agencies, citing typical instances.
B. To show what the legal bases are for the power exercised by courts in attendance enforcement, pointing out their origins and meanings.
C. To evaluate points of adequate functioning and of inadequate functioning.
D. To study the division of duties between the schools and the courts in enforcing attendance.
E. To indicate where improvements may be made in laws and in court procedure.

To attain these ends, recourse was had to the publications of school administrators, to the state school laws, to the state reports of decisions of courts of record, to close contact with the work of the courts in two large cities, and to some transcripts of cases involving a violation of attendance laws adjudicated by the courts. The specific sources of data with which each chapter deals are described within that chapter.

CHAPTER II

THE PLACE OF THE COURTS IN THE ADMINISTRATION OF ATTENDANCE LAWS

SOURCES

The sources consulted for the information in this chapter have been largely the reports of state superintendents of schools, city superintendents of schools, state school surveys, city school surveys, and Children's Bureau Publications. The most recent reports on compulsory attendance available in the library of Teachers College, Columbia University, were examined. They included one hundred forty-eight reports of state superintendents, one hundred seven reports of city superintendents in twenty-five cities in seventeen states, twenty city school surveys, and twelve state school surveys.

DIFFICULTY OF ENFORCEMENT BY LOCAL SCHOOL OFFICIALS

Some of these sources set forth the difficulty of getting attendance cases into court when the charges of violation of the law must be made by local officials. A county superintendent in New Jersey complains that the lax enforcement of the compulsory education law is due to the fact that the attendance officers are local officials, and are unwilling to bring their neighbors into court or even to serve warnings on them.[1] Some of the local attendance officers had refused reappointment. The remedy recommended was the appointment of a county attendance officer for each county. The Commissioner of Education of New Jersey in discussing the ineffectiveness of local enforcement of attendance laws writes:

> It is asserted that there are cases where the attendance officers are appointed with the understanding that they are not to enforce the law to get the children into school and keep them there. . . . One defect of the present law is that the township or district unit is not large enough. The local attendance officer is not likely to enforce the law against men whom

[1] *Annual Report of the Commissioner of Education*, 1920, p. 62.

he calls by their first names, and the result is that the law is laxly enforced or not enforced at all.[2]

What we need is an attendance bureau at Trenton whose sole business would be to give its attention to the prevention of this enormous waste in dollars and cents, to say nothing of the waste in education, which is caused by inadequate enforcement of the compulsory education laws. . . . Steps should be taken at once to remedy what seems to be our greatest defect.[3]

DIFFICULTY OF ENFORCEMENT BY LOCAL COURTS

Not only is there a difficulty in getting cases into court when local officials must be depended on to make the charges, but there is difficulty also in getting enforcement by some of the local courts. This difficulty is suggested in the Nevada report:

The law reads nicely and is effective in the large towns and cities, but in the rural sections it is a dead letter, and will remain so as long as the initiative for the enforcement is in the hands of the trustees. They simply will not swear out warrants for the arrest of their neighbors. . . . If the superintendent had the judicial power to summon the parent or guardian of truant children directly before a district court for adjustment of this trouble, there would be little cause for further complaint.[4]

A similar indictment occurs in the South Dakota report:

Almost entirely the enforcement of the compulsory attendance law is in the hands of the local authorities, who often are not interested in education and in some cases are not in sympathy with it. Hence they do not see their duty clearly when it comes to taking active steps to see that children of school age are regularly in attendance at school. The state should have the right of demanding a change of venue in these cases to the Circuit Court and the penalty provided for by law should be sufficiently severe so that it would not pay from a financial standpoint to keep children out of school to perform various tasks at home. . . . The right to excuse from regular attendance at school should be placed in the hands of the county superintendent rather than in the hands of the district board, except in cases of the larger cities. . . . In many cases, the enforcement of law by local authorities is a failure.[5]

The Kentucky survey found that local officials were not likely to bring attendance cases to court.

School trustees were expected to enforce the law, which, of course, they seldom did or could.[6]

[2] *Annual Report of the Commissioner of Education*, 1919, p. 89.
[3] *Ibid.*, p. 91.
[4] *Biennial Report of the Superintendent of Public Instruction*, 1917-18, p. 59.
[5] *Biennial Report of the Superintendent of Public Instruction*, 1918-20, pp. 10 and 11.
[6] *Kentucky Survey*, 1921, p. 91.

This survey, too, found weakness in the county and magisterial courts as enforcement agencies.

County judges and magistrates are so intimately connected with local affairs, and under so many personal obligations that they cannot be relied on to prosecute their neighbors for failure to send their children to school.[7]

In an investigation of juvenile delinquency in New York, the Children's Bureau concluded that the elimination of the justice of the peace as a judge and probation officer was needed.[8] It gave also an explanation for nonenforcement of the attendance law by local officials.

Town school authorities are in general not inclined to enforce the truancy law, except when obliged to do so by the State Education Department. The explanation is simple—it is often neighborly feeling. Can a man who is a school trustee say to his friend and neighbor—"John, if you keep that boy of yours out of school another day, I'll have you before the justice of the peace (another mutual friend and neighbor) and have you fined ten dollars"? And then, even if this trustee does have the courage of his convictions, perhaps the justice of the peace will not have, and instead of roundly fining neighbor John, will let him off with some good advice. Sometimes the trustees tell the teachers they must accept any excuse that the children bring.[9]

Laxity of enforcement by local courts is suggested in the West Virginia report.

The law, poorly enforced as it has been, has increased attendance very much. It can increase it much more when there can be found in every district a few men who would as willingly be useful as popular and a justice of the peace with some regard for his oath of office.[10]

In the Louisville, Kentucky, report, it is argued that if the law were strongly enforced, the question of school attendance would be largely solved; for while the number of cases in which it was necessary to introduce petitions in court were few in comparison with the total number of cases handled, yet they were critical in regard to their disposition because of the effect which they had upon the school neighborhood from which they came.[11] The Philadelphia report states that the prosecution of parents in the magistrate's court is not the least unpleasant work

[7] *Kentucky Survey,* 1921, p. 92.
[8] Children's Bureau Publication, No. 32, p. 9, 1918.
[9] *Ibid.,* p. 38.
[10] *Biennial Report of State Superintendent of Schools,* 1920, p. 29.
[11] *Louisville City School Report,* 1917-18, p. 155.

which the attendance officers in the course of their official duties are called upon to perform. But it is important that this work should be well done because every court case successfully carried through is thoroughly advertised in the neighborhood of the defendant's home, and has a bracing effect upon careless and indifferent parents. Thus school attendance is improved generally, and much unnecessary work for the school and attendance officer is eliminated. On the other hand, when a defendant is discharged, the failure of the prosecution becomes known, and other parents take the chance of evading the law and the work of enforcement is rendered correspondingly difficult.[12]

The Paducah, Kentucky, report gives instances of lax enforcement by courts.

> Court proceedings were taken against seven parents for failure to comply with the compulsory school law. Two were fined, the others cautioned and dismissed. There has been an improvement in legal procedure in such matters over last year, but a better coöperation and a real interest in enforcing the law on the part of the county court is desirable.[13]

The New Hampshire report states that cases which the local truant officer cannot adjust are referred to the state inspectors. They advise the parents and warn them of the effect of further violation of the law. If the warning is not effective, the parents are brought into court and fined. During the biennium, no case had been presented which the courts had not held to be justified and where fines were not imposed.[14] The North Dakota report states that prosecutions for nonattendance seemed to have a good moral effect.[15] In the California report are given the results of a questionnaire on enforcement of compulsory education sent to each county superintendent. Of the fifty-eight counties, forty-three had no county attendance officer. There were sixty-four prosecutions of parents and ten of employers for violation of the compulsory education law. These resulted in fifty-seven convictions, twenty-four suspended sentences, and six dismissals. The fines amounted to $465.[16]

[12] *Philadelphia City School Report,* 1917, p. 155.

[13] *Paducah City School Report,* 1919-20, p. 12.

[14] *Report of State Board of Education,* 1922, p. 107.

[15] *Fourteenth Biennial Report,* Superintendent of Public Instruction, June 30, 1916, p. 111.

[16] *Fourth Biennial Report,* State Board of Education, 1918-20, p. 71.

ENFORCEMENT AS REVEALED BY SURVEYS

The Providence survey discovered that the court had little, if any, value to prevent or decrease the amount of truancy or non-attendance. It stated that an adequate provision for attendance officers would do much to preclude the necessity for court action.[17] In the Atlanta survey no relationship was found to be existing between the attendance department and the juvenile court, and there had been no coöperation in the past. The attendance officers had brought no cases to the court, although the court expressed a willingness to coöperate with the attendance bureau. The attendance cases that had been brought in the court were brought by other agencies than the attendance bureau.[18] On the other hand, a lack of coöperation by the court was found in Watertown. Over a period of ten years, only one person had been fined in court out of a considerable number of cases arraigned. Such an attitude of the court would result in negligence and discontent by the attendance officer and a disregard of compulsory education laws by parents and children.[19]

The practice in attendance cases in the court at Springfield, Mass., was to impose a fine of fifteen dollars, but to revoke the fine in most cases. No record was found where the fine had been collected. In some of the cases, the children had absences ranging from twelve to one hundred twenty-eight days, and they had been reported by the school principal from eight to fourteen times before they were brought into court.[20] The survey staff recommended that:

> An effort should be made to secure a more strenuous coöperation of the courts. . . . A wholesome fear of court action should always serve as a deterrent to habitual offenders.[21]

In his study of attendance service in fifteen cities, Emmons found that there was a tendency of courts to take a sentimental view of compulsory attendance as applied to children, parents, and employers. He found, too, that in all but two of these cities

[17] *Report of the Survey of Certain Aspects of the Public School System of Providence, R. I., 1923-24*, p. 63.

[18] *Report of the Survey of the Public School System of Atlanta, Ga., 1921-22*, p. 42.

[19] *Report of the Survey of the Schools of Watertown, N. Y., 1924-25*, p. 94.

[20] *Report of the Survey of the Public School System of Springfield, Mass., 1923-24*, p. 45.

[21] *Ibid.*, p. 47.

the attendance department felt powerless to secure such co-operation from the courts as would bring about satisfactory attendance on the part of those who were determined to resist the enforcement of the law. At the same time, he made clear the primary responsibility of the schools, through their attendance service, to present convincing facts to the court so that the court might take intelligent and impartial action.[22]

Summary

1. Appeal to the courts to enforce attendance laws is hindered when the law provides that local officials must bring the charges of violation. Administrators advise that the law should make provision that charges may be brought by county and state officials.
2. Local courts are in many cases found ineffective as means for enforcing the attendance laws. The law should make appeal possible to such courts as county courts, district courts, and circuit courts.
3. The kind of court action secured in attendance cases affects greatly the success of school attendance departments in improving attendance. The attitude of the court and its decisions on the cases brought before it are important factors either in strengthening or in partly nullifying attendance laws.
4. Efficient functioning by courts depends on an adequate and efficient attendance service in the schools.

[22] Emmons, Frederick E. *City School Attendance Service*, pp. 111 and 112.

CHAPTER III

JUDICIAL DECISIONS AFFECTING COMPULSORY ATTENDANCE

SOURCES

It is a function of the courts to render decisions in controverted cases in which compulsory attendance is involved. The sources consulted for cases of this kind in courts of record gave relatively few in number.[1] The cases of courts of record only could be made a subject of study for the reason that such courts alone print a record of their experiences with suit cases in a form that the entire history of a case may later be available for review. Forty-six such recorded cases in all were found. They range in time from the year 1871 to 1925. Most of them have occurred since 1900, thirty-seven, or slightly more than eighty per cent of the cases, having occurred since that time.

CASES BY YEARS

In the following tabulation the years and the number of cases for each year are given. In the twenty-nine years from 1871 to 1900 only nine cases were decided.

Year	Cases	Year	Cases	Year	Cases
1871	1	1901	3	1915	1
1876	1	1902	2	1916	3
1880	1	1903	1	1917	2
1883	1	1904	2	1918	3
1891	1	1906	3	1919	2
1893	1	1909	3	1921	2
1896	1	1911	1	1922	2
1899	1	1912	2	1924	3
1900	1	1914	1	1925	1

[1] The sources for locating cases were the volumes of the *American Digest*, the *American and English Cyclopedia of Law*, the state digests, and the references cited in the court decisions themselves. The judicial decisions of state superintendents and commissioners of education are not included in this study. These officials are not courts, have a limited jurisdiction in making legal decisions, are not specified in attendance laws as having jurisdiction in attendance cases, and have not the power to impose the penalties of fines and imprisonments.

CASES BY STATES

In this list of forty-six cases, only twenty states are represented. By states, the number of cases are as follows:

State	Cases	State	Cases
Pennsylvania	8	Michigan	2
New York	6	Wisconsin	2
Indiana	4	Iowa	1
Ohio	3	Oklahoma	1
Washington	3	Kansas	1
Oregon	2	Massachusetts	1
Virginia	2	Minnesota	1
New Hampshire	2	Illinois	1
Tennessee	2	Texas	1
Missouri	2	North Carolina	1

Pennsylvania and New York together have nearly one-third of all the cases. If only those states are considered which have two or more cases, it is found that thirty-six cases, or nearly eighty per cent of the total, have occurred in eleven states. This indicates that litigation affecting compulsory attendance has been confined to a few states.

A classification of the forty-six cases under the general question that each deals with shows that there are seventeen such questions. Some of them have been dealt with in cases a number of times; some only once. For example, the question of the constitutionality of compulsory education legislation has been a question for judicial decision in four cases. Out of the seventeen questions, seven cover thirty-six of the cases, and ten cover the remaining ten cases. In other words, each of these last ten questions is represented in judicial decisions by only one case.

CONSTITUTIONALITY OF COMPULSORY EDUCATION LEGISLATION

It would be expected that one of the questions which the courts would be required to settle would be the constitutionality of legislation making attendance at school compulsory. Decisions have been rendered on this matter, as stated above, in the courts of four states; namely, Ohio, Indiana, New Hampshire, and Pennsylvania. In every instance, the constitutionality of the compulsory attendance law has been affirmed.

The Ohio Case.—In the Ohio case, the court held that an act to compel children under fourteen years of age to attend school a certain length of time each year was constitutional.[2] The

[2] Quigby v. State, 5 Ohio Cir. Ct. 638. Decided 1891.

right of the legislature under the constitution of the state to pass such a law had been denied by a citizen of the state. He had resisted the law for the purpose of raising the constitutional questions involved and of having them decided in court.

The court stated that since 1877 the principle of the enforced attendance upon school for the children of the state had been a part of the state's legislation as to schools, and up to the time of this case the authority to pass such laws had never been questioned in the courts. The law did not abridge the right or duty of parents to educate their children. It recognized the right and sought to enforce the duty. The law did not interfere with the control or management of private schools. Attendance upon a parochial or other private school was not forbidden. Such attendance was a full compliance with the law, and children in the state who attended parochial or other private schools were not required by the law to attend public schools.

In determining the power of the legislature of the state to enact any particular law, the proper inquiry to make was whether such an exercise of legislative power was clearly prohibited by the constitution of the state. Such prohibition must either be found in express terms or be clearly inferable by necessary implication from the language of the instrument when fairly construed according to its manifest spirit and meaning. If no such prohibition was found, the legislature had the power to enact the law in question. In this respect, the state constitution differed fundamentally from the Constitution of the United States. In the case of the former, it is asked if the power is denied or limited for the legislative department; in the case of the latter, it is asked if the power is expressly given the legislative department.

It was a well-established rule that the courts were not authorized to declare a law unconstitutional and void unless it was clearly in conflict with some of the provisions of the constitution, and every doubt must be clearly resolved in favor of the law. There was no such conflict shown between this law and the constitution. It followed that the legislature had the lawful power to use it, and that each and all of its provisions were binding upon all persons to whom they were applicable. If the law was unwise or oppressive, or unjust, that was good reason why steps should be taken to secure its repeal, or the removal of any of its objectionable features. But it furnished no excuse for a violation of the law.

The claim was made in this case that the statute was unconstitutional because it interfered with the parental authority and the parent's right to direct as to the education of his children. The court argued that as a general rule, the parents are entitled to the custody of their children. In all cases of controverted right to custody, however, the welfare of the minor child was first to be considered. The father's right was not absolute under all circumstances. He might relinquish it by contract, forfeit it by abandonment, or lose it by being in a position of total inability to afford his minor child necessary care and comfort. The legal rights of the parent were to be respected, but the welfare of the minor was of paramount consideration. If necessary to attain the child's welfare, the custody of minor children was to be taken from their parents or refused to them. The authority of the state to assume the guardianship and education of neglected, homeless children, as well as neglected orphans was unquestioned. If the parent was not the proper person to have custody of a child, then the child might be remanded to the authorities of the reform school to remain in the custody of the reform school. The state assumes the right to look after the care and custody of children who are without proper care and custody from their parents.

The state favors the sending, by the parent, of the child to school, either private or otherwise, where he may be taught to perform his duties to the state or be educated so that he may intelligently perform these duties. It is only when the parent forfeits his right to the child, or at least when he shall so forget his duty to the child as to neglect to educate him, or refuse to educate him, or permits him to run at large so that he becomes a disorderly person within the meaning of the law, or when the child, perhaps without the consent of the parent, takes upon himself the right to do so, that the state steps in and by virtue of these statutes compels his attendance at school. The state declares a child who has arrived at that condition to be a disorderly person; it declares that a parent who has not performed his duty to his child properly to educate him within the limits that are prescribed is guilty of a misdemeanor and shall be punished by a fine.

The Indiana Case.—In deciding the constitutionality of the compulsory attendance law in Indiana, the court argued at length the natural rights of parents and the relation of legislative to judicial authority.[3]

The natural rights of a parent to the custody and control of his infant child were subordinate to the power of the state. They might be restricted and regulated by municipal laws. One of the most important natural duties of the parent was his obligation to educate his child. He owed this duty not to the child only, but to the commonwealth. If he neglected to perform it, or willfully refused to do so, he might be coerced by law to execute such civil obligation. The welfare of the child, and the best interests of society required that the state should exert its sovereign authority to secure to the child the opportunity to acquire an education. Statutes making it compulsory upon the parent or guardian, or other person having the custody and control of children, to send them to public or private schools for longer or shorter periods during certain years of the life of such child were not only within the constitutional power of the legislature but were necessary to carry out the express purposes of the constitution itself.

The matter of education was a legitimate function of the state. It was imposed upon the legislature as a duty by imperative provisions of the constitution. How far interference by the state in the education of children should extend was a question, not of constitutional power for the courts, but of expediency and propriety which it was the sole province of the legislature to determine. The judiciary had no authority to interfere with this exercise of legislative judgment. To do so would be to invade the province which was assigned by the constitution exclusively to the lawmaking power.

To carry out the enlightened and comprehensive system of education enjoined by the constitution of the state, a vast fund dedicated exclusively to this purpose had been set apart. No parent had the right to deprive his child of the advantages thus provided and to defeat the purpose of such munificent appropriations.

The New Hampshire Case.—A parent was convicted in a lower court in the New Hampshire case of a violation of the com-

[3] State v. Bailey, 157 Ind. 324. Decided 1901.

pulsory attendance law.[4] He had offered evidence by a physician to show that his child was in feeble health. This evidence was excluded by the court. The parent claimed that this exclusion was an error and appealed to the supreme court of the state. In addition, the constitutionality of the law was attacked on the grounds that it interfered with the natural right of parental dominion and that it was not wholesome and reasonable within the meaning of the article of the constitution which gave the legislature power to make wholesome and reasonable laws.

The supreme court, in reviewing the case and construing the law, reached the following conclusions:

A. The law making attendance at public school of children between eight and fourteen years old compulsory, subject to a penalty except on the excuse of the school board for physical or mental condition or attendance at a private school, was not unconstitutional because it interfered with the natural right of parental dominion.

B. The law making attendance at public school of children of school age all the time such school was in session compulsory, unless excused by the school board, had no reference to occasional or temporary absence.

C. Evidence that a child was in feeble health, that the parent took her from school believing in good faith that her attendance would seriously affect her health, and that he so informed two members of the school board before he took her away, was proper for the jury on the question whether the school board excused her from attendance. The exclusion of such evidence was an error.

D. Whether the compulsory attendance law was wholesome and reasonable within the provision of the constitution giving the legislature power to make wholesome and reasonable laws, which it might judge to be for the benefit and welfare of the state, might not be questioned by the court. The court could only inquire whether the law violated some other constitutional provision.

E. The right of defense of life, liberty, and property was guaranteed by the constitution. The compulsory attendance law would not be construed to require a parent to imperil the life of a child by sending him to school pending delay incident to appli-

[4] State v. Jackson, 71 N.H. 552. Decided 1902.

cation for excuse, or to send him though an excuse was refused, where withdrawing him was apparently reasonably necessary in defense of his life. However, in case of complaint against a parent for withdrawing or detaining his child from school without excuse from the school board, the burden would be upon the accused to show that what he did was apparently necessary in defense of the child's life. Failing, he would be amenable to the statute. Succeeding, he would be exempt from its operation. The statute was intended to secure the attendance of children who were able, and not to confer arbitrary power upon the school board.

In the argument for these decisions, the court affirmed that the education of the citizen was essential to the stability of the state. The constitution declared that knowledge and learning generally diffused through a community were essential to the preservation of a free government. But it did not stop with this abstract statement. It provided that it was the duty of the legislators and magistrates in all future periods of the government to cherish the interest of literature and the sciences and all seminaries and public schools. It being thus the constitutional duty of the legislature to diffuse knowledge and learning through the community, it must be within the constitutional power of the legislature to enforce school attendance to that end. The constitution further provided that full power and authority were given and granted to the legislature, from time to time, to make, ordain, and establish all manner of wholesome and reasonable orders, laws, statutes, ordinances, directions, and instructions, either with penalties or without, so as they be not repugnant or contrary to the constitution, as the legislators might judge for the benefit and welfare of the state, and for the governing and ordering thereof. The court had no control over the question as to whether the compulsory attendance law was wholesome and reasonable. It could not inquire into the policy of the law, or, if the purpose be admitted to be public, whether the supposed public good to be attained was sufficient to justify the legislature. All questions of expediency and all questions respecting the just operation of the law, within the limits prescribed by the constitution, were settled by the legislature when it was enacted.

The law was not unconstitutional merely because in obedience to the mandate of the constitution and for the preservation of a free government it interfered in some measure with the natural right of parental dominion. When men enter into a state of society, they surrender up some of their natural rights to that society in order to secure the protection of others, and subject themselves to innumerable restrictions and regulations for the common good. But the surrender is not absolute. There are certain natural, essential, and inherent rights reserved by the constitution of which the citizen cannot be deprived by legislative enactment: rights paramount to all governmental authority, which no legislation could invalidate or abridge. As a fundamental and essential right, the defense of life, liberty, and property is put by a special guaranty above the altering and repealing power of the legislature. Thus it was held that one might lawfully kill a mink in defense of his geese, notwithstanding the existence of a statute providing that no person shall in any way destroy any mink under penalty of ten dollars for each animal so destroyed. The owner's natural, common-law, and constitutional right of defense existed in full force and vigor, not repealed nor in the slightest degree impaired or modified by the statute. He could exercise that right as fully and freely as if the statute had not been enacted.

If statutory prohibitions and penalties were thus impotent to take away the inherent right of defense when invoked in behalf of one's geese, that must surely be so when the right was resorted to in defense of one's own life or that of his child. For the diffusion of knowledge and learning through the community the legislature had the undoubted right, as against the mere will and pleasure of the parent, to require him to send his child to school. But they could not repeal the natural, common-law, and constitutional right of the parent to do whatever apparently was reasonably necessary to be done in defense of the life of his child. If it was apparently reasonably necessary for a parent to keep or withdraw his child from school in defense of the child's life without first applying for excuse by the school board, the legislature could not compel him to first make such application.

The Pennsylvania Case.—In the Pennsylvania case, the opponents of the law urged its unconstitutionality for the reasons that: (*a*) it was special and class legislation [5]; (*b*) its provisions

[5] Commonwealth v. Edsall, 13 Pa. D. R. 509. Decided 1903.

were burdensome and oppressive; (*c*) it unreasonably deprived a parent of discretion as to the attendance of his child at school; (*d*) the constitution of the state did not confer upon the legislature the right to compel the attendance of children in the common schools of the commonwealth; (*e*) by its title it failed to give notice fairly of compulsory attendance as required by its terms, or of the duties sought to be imposed upon parents respecting the compulsory attendance of children; (*f*) it deprived parents of their rights to protect children from danger by withdrawing them from school when their safety seemed to require it; (*g*) it was in contravention of the provisions of the Fourteenth Amendment of the Constitution of the United States.

The decision of the court was directed towards a few of the objections advanced and ignored the others. It affirmed that the judicial department of the government could not give relief against enactments which were deemed burdensome and oppressive, if no other valid reason could be shown. Those who objected to their operation must be able to point to some section of the constitution containing a prohibition upon the legislative authority to pass them. The rules which had been set for the interpretation of powers under the federal constitution were not applicable to the organic law of the several states. In the former case, no powers could be exercised which were not directly granted or plainly implied; but all such authority not thus delegated was reserved to the states or the people. The constitution of any state allowed to its legislature every power which it did not prohibit.

Statutes under the police power of the state were exempt from the prohibition of the Fourteenth Amendment. In considering the validity of an enactment of a state legislature upon the police power, the court inquired whether the regulation or classification had been designed to subserve some reasonable public purpose, or was a mere device or excuse for an unjust discrimination, or for the oppression or spoliation of a particular class. Any regulation of the internal affairs of the state fairly serving a valid police purpose and reasonably exercised for the community at large would be upheld. But if it were arbitrary and had no substantial relation to the health, morals, peace, or welfare of the community, it would be nullified.

A large discretion was vested in the legislature to determine not only what the interests of the public required, but what measures were necessary to protect them.

The Supreme Court of the United States had recently given firm expression to the doctrine that in the consideration of cases where the provisions of the Fourteenth Amendment were invoked, it must not be forgotten that the law was a progressive science which must always construe a settled principle with such expansive interpretation that it would meet advancing and changing conditions; that what was once sufficient for the public safety or welfare might no longer meet the requirement; and just as the necessity grew by the development of science and creation of new agencies, so did the occasion for additional sanctions by legislation.

The acts of the legislature which established the house of refuge wherein children within a certain age might be committed and taken from parental custody for their interests and education were not in conflict with the bill of rights. The public had a paramount interest in the virtue and knowledge of its members, and of strict right the business of education belonged to it. The right of parental control was a natural but not an inalienable one. It was not excepted by the declaration of rights out of the subjects of ordinary legislation. As to abridgement of indefeasible rights by confinement of the person, it was no more than what was borne to a greater or less extent in every school.

Whenever the state in the exercise of its judgment determined that a system of compulsory education was essential for the welfare of the community at large, it was not forbidden by federal restraint.

The attendance of the pupil at school was to be continuous, unless he was excused by the boards of control upon satisfactory evidence. The Boards, not the parents, were by the statutes constituted the judges of what were sufficient mental, physical, or other urgent reasons for the absence or for the irregular attendance of the child.

Summary

1. The constitutionality of compulsory education enactments has been upheld in four different states in every one of the four cases that have been tried. For nearly twenty-five

years, the constitutionality of such a law has not been questioned in the courts of any state.

2. The courts have decided that such legislation is within the discretion of the state legislatures, no state constitutions specifically prohibiting such enactments.
3. Such legislation comes under the police power of the legislature for the promotion of the health, morals, peace, or welfare of the community.
4. The legislature has the right to limit parental authority and dominion, and may enact laws compelling attendance at school of children within definite ages and for a definite period of time each year.
5. Every state in the union has now enacted such legislation.[6] This represents a remarkable achievement in change of viewpoint with regard to education, since the days of Horace Mann's service as secretary of the state board of education in Massachusetts. Even in that most progressive state educationally of that time a general compulsory attendance law could probably not have been enforced.[7]

LEGALITY OF RULES AND REGULATIONS AFFECTING ATTENDANCE

The power of school boards to make rules and regulations that enforce attendance at school has been a matter for decision by the courts. The sources consulted gave reference to four cases of this kind in the states of Iowa, Vermont, Missouri, and Illinois.

The Iowa Case.—A school board had provided for the government of the schools under its direction a set of rules among which were the following:

> Rule 10.—Any pupil who is absent six half-days in any consecutive four weeks, and two times tardy, shall be counted as one absent, unless detained by sickness or other unavoidable cause, shall be suspended from the schools until the end of the term, or until reinstated by the superintendent or board.[8]
>
> Rule 11.—Teachers may require absence and tardiness to be certified to by parent or guardian, in writing or personally, or by special messenger. All lessons lost on account of absence may be made up at the discretion of the teacher.

[6] Bermejo, F. V. *The School Attendance Service in American Cities*, p. 19.
[7] Ensign, F. C. *Compulsory School Attendance and Child Labor*, p. 49.
[8] Burdick v. Babcock, 31 Iowa 562. Decided 1871.

The court decided: first, that under the constitution and laws of Iowa it was competent for boards of school directors to provide by rules that pupils might be suspended from the schools in case they should be absent or tardy, except for sickness or other unavoidable cause, a certain number of times within a fixed period; and second, that such rules were reasonable and proper for the government of schools, and their enforcement was essential to their well-being and the success of pupils therein.

In this case, the court had before it the facts relative to two pupils whose school attendance these rules affected. One pupil had been suspended from the public schools of the district under Rule 10. The teacher informed the father of his son's absence and tardiness, and told him that the boy would be reinstated if a proper excuse were rendered for him and assurance given that the acts would not be repeated. The father informed the teacher that his son had been kept at home to perform certain labors, and was for that reason absent and tardy at school; that he could give no assurance against the repetition of the fault, and claimed the right to detain his child from school at any time for like reasons, and, notwithstanding the rule and action under it, to send him to the school.

The other pupil had been kept from school by her parents for the purpose of being taken by them upon a visit. The parents represented that, as they were in humble circumstances, they could not leave their child at home when they made a visit, and for that reason found it necessary to take the child with them. The absence for which the child was suspended was her second offense of the kind against the rules of the school.

The case came to the supreme court of the state on appeal from the judgment of a district court. The parents of the pupils had sued the school directors and the teacher, claiming damages for the suspension of the children, and praying that the school directors and teacher be restrained from enforcing the rules and be required by proper order to admit the children into the school. The judgment of the district court was in favor of the parents.

The supreme court was not unanimous in its decision, one judge delivering a dissenting opinion. In the prevailing argument, the court stated that the case turned upon the power of the board of directors to establish and enforce rules like Rule 10. The plaintiff insisted that the rule was unreasonable and in its enforcement operated oppressively and unjustly towards the pupils. The point presented for the determination of the court was narrowed to the single question: Was the rule under which the children were suspended from the school reasonable and proper?

The object of public schools as established by the laws was to secure education to the children of the state. The intention of the law was not that the children should at certain times or on certain days be simply gathered together, but that, when assembled, they should be instructed. Their progress in learning was the grand object of the law. It intended that the school should be so conducted that the children should make the most rapid advances possible in the acquisition of knowledge and mental discipline.

Any rule of the school not subversive of the rights of the children or parents, or in conflict with humanity and the precepts of divine law, which tended to advance the object of the law in establishing public schools, must be considered reasonable and proper.

It required but little experience in the instruction of children to convince anyone that the only means which would assure progress in their studies was to secure their attendance—the application of the powers of their minds to the studies in which they were instructed. Unless a pupil's mind was open to receive instruction, the effort of the teacher to lead him forward in learning would be vain. The application of the mind was secured by interesting the child in his studies. This could not be done if he was at school one day and at home the next, if a recitation was omitted or a lesson left unlearned at the whim or convenience of parents. A child, to be interested, must be able to understand the subject in which he was instructed. If he had failed to prepare previous lessons, he would not understand the one which the teacher explained to him. If he was required to do double duty and prepare a previous lesson, omitted in order to make a visit, or do an errand at home, in addition to preparing the lesson of the day, he would fail to master both and would become discouraged. The inevitable consequence was that his interest flagged and he was unable to apply the powers of his mind to the studies before him. The rule requiring constant and prompt attendance was for the good of the pupil, and operated to secure the very objects the law had in view in establishing public schools. It was therefore reasonable and proper.

In another view, the rule was required by the best interest of all the pupils of the school. Irregular attendance of pupils not only retarded their own progress, but it also interfered with the progress of those pupils who were regular and prompt. The whole class might be annoyed and hindered by the imperfect recitations of one who had failed to prepare his lessons on account of absence. The class must endure and suffer the blunders of the irregular pupil, the promptings and reproofs which he provoked, —all resulting from failure to prepare lessons which should have been studied when the child's time was occupied by direction of the parent in work or visiting.

Tardiness, arriving late, was a direct injury to the whole school. The confusion of hurrying to seats, the gathering together of books and accessories by tardy ones, at a time when all should be at study, could not fail greatly to impede the progress of those who were regular and prompt in attendance. Requiring prompt and regular attendance was demanded by the good of the whole school. While it might be admitted that absence and tardiness were acts committed out of school hours, yet as their effects and consequences operated upon the school—the pupils when assembled for instruction—they were therefore subject to control by rules for the government of the schools. If the effects of acts done out of schoolhouses reached within the schoolroom during the school hours and were detrimental to good order and the best interest of the pupils, it was evident that such acts might be forbidden. Truancy, it is true, was a fault committed away from school, but it could not be pretended that it could not be reached for correction by the school board and teachers. The view that acts, to be within the authority of the school board and teachers for discipline and correction, must be done within school hours, was narrow and without regard to the spirit of the law and the best interest of the common schools.

The argument was advanced that the rule interfered with parental authority. The court's view was that the services and society of the child during school hours could not be at the disposal of the father. Neither had the parent the right to interfere with the order of the school or the progress of other pupils by sending his own child at times and in condition that would prove an annoyance and hindrance to others.

The argument was advanced, too, that the rule visited upon the child punishment for the parent's offense. The court regarded this completely answered by the consideration that the parent's act was an injury to the whole school. If the education of the child were compulsory upon parents who could be reached by proper penalties, the child could be relieved from the hardship of expulsion. As the law was, no other means could be devised for enforcing the rule requiring regular and prompt attendance than the penalty of expulsion.

The judge who delivered the dissenting opinion argued that Rule 10 was not a rule for the government of the school, but for the regulation of parents and guardians who sent pupils to the public schools, and also for the government of the pupils out of and away from school. The parent, whose authority the child must obey, deprived him, necessarily or otherwise, of a portion of his school privileges by keeping him at home for a few days. Then the school directors, for that cause alone, deprived him of all its benefits—such was the working of the rule in these cases.

The Vermont Case.—The Vermont case related to the right of the prudential committee of a school district to make and enforce rules that excluded children from school for the rest of the term, if, contrary to the rules, they were absent without the consent of the committee, even though such absence was pursuant to the command of their parents and by direction of their pastor for the purpose of attending religious services.[9]

Parents had asked the prudential committee of the village to exempt their children from attendance at school on holy days. This request was made about ten minutes before the beginning of the forenoon session of school. It involved about one hundred and fifty children out of a total enrollment of about six hundred. The prudential committee refused. About sixty children stayed out on that day. When they applied for admission to school next day, they were told they could not return without an assurance from their parents, or their pastor, that in the future they would comply with the rules of the school not to absent themselves without permission of the prudential committee on

[9] Ferriter and Others v. Tyler and Others, 48 Vt. 444. Decided 1876.

cause shown. The committee assured the children and many of their parents and also the pastor that if the schools would not again be interrupted in like manner, they would gladly re-admit the children. The pastor and parents refused to comply with such a proposal, and claimed that on all days which they regarded as holy, they might as a matter of right take their children from the schools without any regard to the rules thereof, or to the injury they thereby did them; that there were eight or ten such holy days in each year, six or seven of which usually occurred when the schools were in session. Never before had children of this faith been taken from school nor had any claim of right to do so been made. Laboring men of this faith, and women of the village, were generally at their places of business and labor during the day, and labored as on other days. Four years before, a pastor of this church had asked to withdraw children to attend service, but, on being denied, he withdrew the request and held services at his church at hours that would not conflict with the sessions of the schools.

The church involved in this suit claimed that the enforcing of the rules of suspension by the committee upon the children violated their rights under Article III of the state constitution, guaranteeing the right to worship God according to the dictates of their conscience. It violated also the legal right of the parents to control their children in the matter of attending the public schools of the district, as against the right of the committee in the same behalf.

The court held that the action of the committee in refusing to exempt children from attending school on holy days did not touch nor affect the worship of Almighty God by the members of that church. It did not touch nor affect their religious sentiments or peculiar mode of religious worship. It did not interfere with nor control the rights of conscience in the free exercise of religious worship.

The principle stood out so plainly as not to be a matter for debate, even if it were not expressly conceded, that schools, in order to realize the intent of the constitution in their behalf, must be subjected to system and order under established rules. Hence, the law charged the committee with the duty of adopting all requisite measures for the inspection, examination, and regulation of the schools and the improvement of the pupils in learning. If it were granted that parents and others might, upon their own respective reasons, control the attendance of the pupils, as against the official right of the committee in that behalf, practically the ground of system, order, and improvement had no existence. For the parents and guardians of the pupils might, each on his own motion, and on his own notions, withhold their children from the schools.

When the matter of conscience as against the requirements of the law was brought to the test, the practical result of what the church in this case claimed was shown to be so impracticable, not otherwise to characterize it, as to preclude further discussion. A Catholic citizen, a Jew, a Methodist, or a Seventh-day Baptist on jury duty would hardly regard it as a violation of his right of conscience to be refused permission to attend divine service.

Considering the question of the legal right of the parent's control, or the prerogative of parents to control their children as pupils as against the right of the committee to make and enforce the rule in question, the court held that the statutes of the state charged the committee with the duty of "adopting all requisite measures" as before stated. The committee adopted rules for the regulation of the schools and for the improvement of the pupils in learning. The rule in question was for the purpose of inducing and enforcing constancy in attendance. That such constancy was essential to such improvement was not debatable. That such attendance was required as a matter of regulation, in order to make the necessary classification of the scholars in reference to age, capacity, studies, and proficiency was not debatable. Those who attended constantly could not be required to linger in order that the inconstant might keep along with them; nor could such inconstant scholars keep equal poll with those who attended constantly. The rule was such as was contemplated by the statute so far as the purpose of it was concerned. That purpose was indispensable to the attainment of the object and end proposed by the statutes both as to the individual scholar, and as to all the others who might be affected by his attendance and absence. The rule had been in operation for more than ten years. The children of the parents of the church concerned were subjected to its operation in the present instance. That could not be termed unlawful.

If the parents had the right to control the attendance of their children as against that rule, then the committee had not the right to maintain and enforce such rule. The court was not prepared to sanction a view of this subject that would subordinate the authority of the committee in the matter of the attendance of registered scholars to the will of parents. On the other hand, the court did not hesitate to hold and declare as matter of law that in this respect the citizen was in subordination to the lawful rules for the regulation of schools and the improvement of scholars in learning. This was for the same fundamental reason that he was in subordination to the statutes themselves on that or any other subject. It was no more his right to defy and disregard any statute that affected him as a citizen in respect to schools, or any other subject involving the common weal, as it is provided for under the constitution by the legislation of the state.

The rule in question and the enforcement of it were subject to the judgment of the courts as between the parties to the suit. It was easy to suppose cases in which such enforcement would be beyond the lawful right of the committee. The rule itself, in terms and interest, contemplated exclusion as a penalty only where permission to be absent was withheld for want of reasonable cause shown. In case of casual sickness of the pupil, of sickness or death in the family, of some catastrophe like fire or flood; in case of various incidents of current life, giving occasion for temporary absence, the enforcement of the penalty of exclusion would, under such circumstances, be adjudged to be unauthorized under the statutes and law by which the subject is governed.

The Missouri Case.—The question in the Missouri case was whether Rule 11, adapted and enforced by the board of the school district, was a legal one.[10] The rule was:

> Any pupil absent six half days in four consecutive weeks, without satisfactory excuse, shall be suspended from school.

The court stated the argument of the plaintiff in the case, who opposed the rule, to the effect that occasional absences from school on the part of the pupil, or truancy as it was familiarly termed, was of no importance to anyone except the pupil or his parents. Its indulgence was, therefore, not to be attended with

[10] King v. Jefferson City School Board, 31 Mo. 628. Decided 1880.

such punishment as suspension or expulsion from the school entirely. Every child had a right to go to the public school, and that right could not be taken away by a rule of the board. Such a rule was subversive of the object of our system of common schools, which was designed to throw open and leave open the doors of the school to all children of the proper age, and to give them the opportunity of acquiring such education as would fit them for the after duties of life. This, the court said, was true, but this right of attending school necessarily required, when the school was joined, and whilst such attendance continued, a submission to the regulations of the school.

Concerning the argument of the plaintiff that the pupil was at liberty to be absent when he pleased and that such absence was a matter solely between him and his parents, the court stated that the studies in our public schools were classified according to the ages and advancement of the scholars. The continued or repeated absences of one of a class not only was injurious to the absentee, but, if allowed beyond a certain point, was calculated to demoralize those who attended and to derange the orderly instructions of the teacher. Taxes were not collected to pay teachers to sit in front of empty benches or to hunt up truant boys. Absences without excuse were the fault of the parents, whose business it was to see that the attendance of their children was regular, unless prevented by causes which would be an excuse under the rule.

The Illinois Case.—The directors of an Illinois school district prepared, as they were required by law to do, what they conceived to be necessary rules for the regulation and government of the school.[11] The rules were printed and furnished to the teachers, and the teachers gave to each pupil attending school a printed copy of the rules.

One rule was:

> Any pupil who shall be absent six half-days without a valid excuse will be liable to suspension from study, and no pupil thus suspended shall be restored without permission from the board.

Another rule was:

> All pupils will be required to bring written excuses from their parents to teachers for absence, and such excuses must be satisfactory and reasonable; otherwise it will not be granted.

[11] Churchill v. Fewkes, 13 Ill. App. 520. Decided 1883.

A pupil in this district was absent from school two weeks in violation of these rules. When she returned to school she was asked by her teacher if she had been sick. She replied she had not been sick and declined to give any reason for her absence. The teacher called her attention to the rules, and informed her it would be necessary to bring a written excuse from her mother. After several days the principal and teacher wrote polite letters to the mother calling attention to the rules as prepared by the board, and what their duty was in the matter. No reply was made, and after four or five days the child was suspended. The mother brought suit against two school directors and the teachers for damages. In the circuit court, she was awarded damages of three dollars against one director and the teachers.

The case was appealed to the appellate court, which reversed the decision. This court held that the directors and teachers could have had but one object, and that was that the school should be conducted in such a way as would be most beneficial to the people of the district. The rule in question was not a hard or harsh one. It did not of itself indicate any sinister or malevolent purpose or wicked force on the part of the directors. It did not trench upon the rights or dignity of any one. The court was utterly unable to understand how this simple rule or regulation requiring the pupil in certain cases to bring a written excuse from its parents to the teacher was an attack upon or an abridgment of any inalienable rights of citizens of this country. It was a simple regulation, existing no doubt in many of the schools of the country, that of itself was not wicked, willful, nor malicious, and the action of the directors as well as of the teachers in the premises absolutely precluded the idea of willfulness or malice on their part.

Summary

In the matter of the legality of rules and regulations enforcing regular and prompt attendance, the courts have upheld the following views:

1. Rules requiring regular and prompt attendance are reasonable and proper and in the interest both of individual pupils and of the school as a whole. If school authorities apply such rules unreasonably or improperly, the judgment of the courts could be sought.

2. A parent's authority could not be permitted to stand in

the way of the school progress of his own child, or with the order and progress of other children. The absence of a pupil was not a matter solely between him and his parents; it affected the welfare of the whole school.

3. Neither parents nor pastors of churches could claim the right to keep children from school for church services without the consent of the school authorities. The enforcement of a rule of regular attendance by the school authorities was not construed as an interference with constitutional guarantees as to right of religious worship.

4. School authorities might by rule require parents to send written excuses for their children's absence, and these excuses must be satisfactory and reasonable in the judgment of the school authorities. Such a requirement was not an abridgment of any inalienable right of citizens.

5. Rules of school boards for securing prompt and regular attendance had the effect of law and were binding on a citizen as any statute.

6. Taxing the man with means to support public schools justified compelling a man with children of school age to send them promptly and regularly to school.

7. The last of the decisions on this subject was delivered more than forty years ago. The necessity for rules and regulations by local authorities to compel attendance has been obviated by state-wide laws on compulsory attendance. These laws provide punishment for the parent instead of expulsion from school for the pupil. By 1917-18, forty-two states required consecutive attendance when children had once enrolled, and twenty-eight required such attendance for the full term.[12] Specific provision for penalizing parents is made in thirty-five of the present state attendance laws. It is obvious that a wide extension has been made in the application of compulsory requirements, in consideration of the fact that the making of rules and regulations by local authorities was optional.

8. Provisions for enforcing promptness, which is the opposite of tardiness, are still matters for local rules and regulations in all states but one.[13] California provides that a pupil tardy three times without valid excuse may be reported as a truant.[14]

[12] Ross, F. A. *School Attendance in the United States*, p. 22.

[13] State Attendance Laws.

[14] California School Laws, 1923.

9. Specific provisions are made for time off for religious instruction or observance of church ordinances in five states. In the other forty-three states, this is a matter of regulation by local school authorities. The decision in the Vermont case, cited above, has therefore wide application at the present time. The states that have state regulation in this matter are Michigan, Minnesota, South Dakota, West Virginia, and Iowa.[15]

COMPULSORY ATTENDANCE AND VACCINATION

Eleven cases have reached the courts of record in which the relation of compulsory attendance to vaccination was involved. There are more cases than are found under any other classification of this chapter. This indicates that here has been a matter for much controversy and consequent litigation. Cases are reported from seven states: namely, Pennsylvania, New York, Ohio, Michigan, Minnesota, Missouri, and Washington. Each state reports one case, except Pennsylvania, which reports four, and New York, which reports two.

The Pennsylvania Case.—In a Pennsylvania case, the parent of a child had been convicted in a justice of the peace court for an offense against the compulsory education law and had been fined two dollars and costs, after his child had been refused admittance at school upon refusal to bring a certificate of vaccination.[16] The case was appealed to the district court where the judgment of the justice of the peace was reversed.

The district court stated that the compulsory education act, by its terms, did not make it obligatory upon the defendant to obtain a certificate of vaccination. His sole duty prescribed by it was to send his son to school. He did this. The teacher refused the son admission simply because he did not present a certificate. There was nothing in the statute making vaccination mandatory in any case. Neither did it require the child to produce a certificate that it had been successfully vaccinated or had had smallpox. In order to sustain the judgment of the justice of the peace, it would be necessary to say that the defendant was obliged by the terms of the statute to procure, and his son to present, a certificate. This the court could not do. The defendant made a complete answer to the commonwealth

[15] State Attendance Laws.
[16] Commonwealth v. Smith, 9 Pa. D. R. 625. Decided 1900.

when he showed that he had sent his son to school until he was denied admission by the teacher.

The Michigan Case.—The board of education of Kalamazoo, Michigan, had enacted this rule in 1894:

> No pupil shall be admitted into any public school, who cannot furnish satisfactory evidence that he or she has been vaccinated or otherwise secured against smallpox; and no pupil affected with any contagious disease, or coming from a house where such a disease exists shall be allowed to remain in any public school.[17]

A parent who had three children aged eleven, nine, and seven, respectively, secured a mandamus in the circuit court to compel the board of education to admit his children to the public schools. The board appealed to the supreme court.

Opinion in the supreme court was divided on this case, two judges filing a dissenting opinion. The conclusion of their argument was that the board had the power to make the rule quoted, and that such a rule was a reasonable regulation. The prevailing opinion, however, was not of that view. It held that the children were in good health, of school age, had not gotten the smallpox, and had not been exposed to it. The law of the state made it their duty to attend school, and it was the duty of the parent to send them. In case he failed to do so, he might be subjected to fine or imprisonment or both in the discretion of the court. The effect of the rule by the board was to compel the vaccination of the children or subject them and the parents to the penalty of the law. The practical result, if this rule could be sustained, was to give the board of education the right to compel vaccination. If the rule were that during the prevalence of the smallpox in the city the children could not attend school unless vaccinated, a very different result would be reached. These epidemics never lasted long, and the parent and the child might well say, if they desired, they would absent themselves from school during the epidemic, and this could be done without their being lawbreakers. Children infected with or exposed to smallpox might be temporarily excluded, or the school be temporarily suspended, but, like the exercise of similar power in other cases, such power was justified by the emergency, and, like the necessity which gave rise to it, ceased when the necessity ceased. Without a law making vaccination compulsory, or pre-

[17] Matthews v. Board of Education, 127 Mich. 530. Decided 1901.

scribing it upon grounds deemed sufficient by the legislature as necessary to the public health as a condition of admission to or attendance upon the public schools, neither the state board of health nor any local board had any power to make or enforce a rule or order having the force of a general law in the respects mentioned.

There was no statute in the state authorizing compulsory vaccinations, nor any statute which required vaccination as one of the conditions of the right or privilege of attending the public schools. Lawfully to exclude children from the city schools for the cause relied on required such a change in the existing law as the legislature alone could make—a change that should make vaccination of pupils compulsory, or at least prescribe it as a condition of the right or privilege of attending the public schools generally, or during the occurrence of certain emergencies.

The legislature of Michigan had not undertaken to give the school board power, when no epidemic of contagious disease existed or was imminent in the district, to pass a general, continuing rule which would have the effect of a general law excluding all pupils who would not submit to vaccination.

The Minnesota Case.—A mandamus was brought in the supreme court of Minnesota to compel the board of education of St. Paul to admit a child of compulsory school age, and a resident of the city, to the public schools of the city.[18] She had been refused admission because she had not complied with certain regulations of the board requiring pupils to be vaccinated. The case had been decided in favor of the board in the lower court, and the father of the child had appealed.

The counsel for the father did not contend that the legislature did not have power to compel vaccination; nor that it might not delegate such power to municipal authorities. His main contention was that the legislature had never conferred the power upon the board of education, the common council, or the health officers of the city of St. Paul, and, further, if it were shown that authority had been so conferred, that such authority did not appear ever to have been put into operation by them, and was not acted on by the board in this case.

The court, in supporting the conclusions of the lower court, held that the principle in question in the case was whether such

[18] State Ex. Rel. Freeman v. Zimmerman, 86 Minn., 353. Decided 1902.

authority had been conferred. While none of the provisions in the statutes expressly authorized municipal authorities or health officers to require children to be vaccinated as a condition precedent to their admission to the public schools, yet the court had no hesitation in holding that the legislature intended to confer such power upon them.

With reference to the relation of the case to compulsory attendance the court said that the statutes of the state provided that admission to the public schools should be free to all persons of a defined age and residence; that any parent having control of any child of school age was expressly required to send such child to school; that all teachers were required to receive them; that if any child of such school age was denied admission, or suspended, or expelled, without sufficient cause, the board or other officers might be fined. But all these statutory provisions must be construed in connection with, and subordinate to, the statutes on the subject of the preservation of the public health and the prevention of the spread of contagious diseases. The welfare of the many was superior to that of the few, and, as the regulations compelling vaccination were intended and enforced solely for the public good, the rights conferred thereby were primary and superior to the rights of any pupil to attend the public schools.

The Washington Case.—On October 30, 1908, the board of directors of Seattle school district, Seattle, Washington, at the suggestion of the commissioner of health of the city, and the medical society of the county, adopted a resolution requiring all pupils desirous of attending the public schools of the district to be successfully vaccinated as a condition precedent to their right to attend school; further directing that the resolution be not enforced against anyone whose condition of health was such as to render it unsafe for him to undergo vaccination.[19] Under the provisions of this resolution, the minor son of a resident of the district was excluded from the schools of the district solely because he refused to submit to vaccination. The father appealed to the superior court of the county for a writ of mandamus against the board to compel them to admit his son to the school. To his application the board made a return in which they gave as reasons for excluding the son the resolution above mentioned,

[19] State Ex. Rel. McFadden v. Sharrock, 55 Wash. 208. Decided 1902.

together with the recommendations on which it was founded; the fact that smallpox then existed to a greater or less extent in the city of Seattle, and was epidemic in a mild form in many of the near-by cities; that the minor son of the appellant refused to be vaccinated, and the parents refused to cause or permit him to be vaccinated, and that to permit him to attend school would be a menace to good health; and, further, that by virtue of the laws of the state the board was clothed with power, and it was the duty of the board to require successful vaccination as a condition to school attendance, whenever in their judgment conditions demanded the exercise of the power. To this return the appellant demurred on the grounds: first, that the act of the legislature on which the resolution of the board was founded was unconstitutional; second, that it was repealed by a subsequent statute enforcing attendance; and, third, that it was too indefinite to be capable of enforcement. The superior court held the return to be sufficient, and overruled the demurrer. The appellant then elected to stand on his demurrer, whereupon the court issued a judgment dismissing the application. The case was then appealed to the state supreme court.

The court quoted the clause in the law under which the board had acted as follows:

> Every board of directors shall have power, and it shall be their duty to require successful vaccination as a condition of school membership and to provide free vaccination to all who are unable to pay for the same.

The clause in question did not empower the board of directors of the district to provide for compulsory vaccination. The appellant might or might not, as suited his desire, require his son to be vaccinated. The act did no more than provide that the board might make vaccination a necessary condition precedent to attendance upon the public schools. It stood on the same plane as the provisions contained in the act for the exclusion of those afflicted with infections or contagious diseases, or those who resided in houses wherein such diseases were prevalent. In other words, it defined the class of persons who might be permitted to attend the schools created by the act.

The contention that this act was repealed by the subsequent statute of March 16, 1907, which provided for the compulsory education of children was untenable. There was no express repeal of one statute by the other, nor was there such a conflict between them as to work a repeal by implication. If the later statute required compulsory attendance on the public schools, the two statutes taken together might require compulsory vaccination. But even in that case, there would be no repeal of the former by the latter; the legislature had power to require all minors to attend the public schools, and to require them to be vaccinated before so attending. Nor was the statute void because it made no allowance for those physically incapable of vaccinations. It was not presumed that the legislature intended to require as a condition of its right to attend the public schools, the vaccination of a child whose condition of health was such that the operation would endanger its life or injuriously affect it mentally or physically. It was presumed that exceptions were intended in favor of such individuals, and if the officers having in charge the execution of the statute refused to recognize an exception in such a case, the courts could be appealed to to compel such recognition.

It was objected that the statute was too indefinite to be capable of enforcement. This was founded on the fact that it requires "successful vaccination," and no definition of the term was furnished by the statutes. The board of directors construed the statute to mean that a person was successfully vaccinated when the customary reaction was obtained by the operation, or when three operations had been performed without obtaining reaction. This was a common-sense construction, and the court approved it.

The court found no objection to the statute itself, nor to the manner in which it was being enforced.

The Missouri Case.—In a Missouri case, it was held that the parents of a school child were not guilty of violating the compulsory school attendance law in refusing to have their child vaccinated in accordance with a rule of the directors, which was a condition precedent to the right of children to attend school during a smallpox epidemic existing or threatened in the district.[20]

On December 4, 1908, a board of education made this order:

> Whereas it has come to the knowledge of the board of education that smallpox exists within the school district; that they deem it necessary that all children attending school, who have not been vaccinated, must be vaccinated within thirty days.

[20] State Ex. Rel. O'Bannon v. Cole, 220 Mo. 697. Decided 1909.

On January 8, 1909, the board made an additional order:

The board will not accept a certificate of vaccination, unless the physician does state that the child has been vaccinated with vaccine virus, and all children who have had smallpox must bring a certificate from the physician in attendance to that effect; and where such certificate cannot be procured, then the parent or guardian must make affidavit that such child has had the smallpox. Any child who has been vaccinated as many as two times without taking, a certificate from the physician will be accepted.

On January 12, 1909, the board passed this resolution:

No certificate of vaccination shall be received unless the same states that the person was vaccinated externally with vaccine virus.

Under these orders, the children of a resident taxpayer of the district were excluded from the schools of the district because they had not been vaccinated as required. The father instituted action by mandamus in the circuit court of the county to compel the board to reinstate his children as pupils in the schools, and to cancel and annul the orders of the board.

The evidence showed that smallpox had been prevalent in the district for at least eight years; that at the time the first order was made, there were twenty-seven cases of smallpox in the district; that a year or so previous smallpox had been so prevalent that the state board of health threatened to take charge of the district; that there had been five hundred to six hundred cases within the past eight years.

Upon the trial in the circuit court the alternative writ of mandamus was made permanent, and by the judgment and decree of the court the orders and resolution of the board of education quoted above were declared null and void, and the board was directed to set them aside, and forthwith admit the excluded children to school. Judgment also went against the board for costs. The board appealed to the supreme court of the state.

This court held that the board had power, according to the revised statutes of 1899, "to make all needful rules and regulations for the organization, grading and government in their school district—said rules to take effect when a copy of the same, duly signed by order of the board, was deposited with the district clerk, whose duty it would be to transmit, forthwith, a copy of the same to the teachers employed in the schools; said rules might be amended or repealed in like manner." The court had no doubt that in the event of a threatened epidemic of smallpox, school boards could pass a rule excluding all pupils who had not been vaccinated.

The father of the excluded children contended that by reason of the compulsory school act of 1905, the rules in question would force him to violate that law, and that under that law the rules enforced by the school board were void. The court asserted that this act in no way affected these rules. In the first place, there could be no prosecution of a parent for failing to send his child to school under the act of 1905 until after an officer of the school district had notified him to send such child, and then if he failed, a prosecution could be had. The father in the case was in no danger of violating the law. The act made it a misdemeanor to violate its provisions, and the court had yet to hear of a criminal case wherein a defendant was convicted of willfully violating a law when in fact he had manifested the disposition that this father had to comply with the strict letter of the law. The act of the school board, in excluding the children whose officer must initiate the prosecution by giving notice, would be an absolute defense. Beyond all this, the compulsory act of 1905 must be construed with the whole body of the school law, and when so construed it could be made to harmonize therewith to the end that there would be no violation of the law.

The Ohio Case.—In an Ohio case a parent sent his child to a public school and was willing to continue to do so, but the child was excluded for failure to comply with a rule of the board of education requiring vaccination, adopted under authority of state law which provided that the board of each district might make and enforce such rules to secure vaccination of pupils attending school as in its opinion the safety and interest of the public require. The court held that the parent was not liable to conviction under the compulsory education act which provided that every parent having charge of any child between the ages of eight and fourteen years who should fail to place such child in school should upon conviction be fined.[21]

The court argued that the compulsory education act was obviously intended to meet the cases where the parent was indifferent to the attendance of the child and made no effort to cause the child to attend the schools. The act was certainly not intended to be used as a means of enforcing any rule which the

[21] State v. Turney, 31 Ohio C.C.R. 222. Decided 1909.

board in the plenitude of its general powers might see fit to adopt. Such a construction would give the board of education the power by indirect means of criminal legislation not only against the pupil, but also against the parents. To so hold required clear legislative expression, and the authority could not be sustained by inference or implication. The accused was to have the benefit of the doubt.

There was a well-recognized principle that acts derogatory of common right and abridging personal liberty were, like penal laws, to be strictly construed in favor of the citizen, and that the legislature alone as the sovereign power could declare the necessity, and it must do so expressly; otherwise the intention would not be inferred. Under the rule of strict construction, the delegation of power to the board to "make and enforce" rules did not contemplate any other penalties for a violation of the rule than those which the board had authority to inflict; namely, suspension or exclusion from the schools of which they had control.

The counsel for the board of education contended that the exclusion of the child from the public schools did not relieve the parent from the obligation under the compulsory education law of seeking its admission into a private or parochial school. In reply, the court said that it was true that the parent was required by the act to send his child to a public, private, or parochial school, yet the election was with the parent. The character of the system of public schools and the manner in which they were sustained did not justify the court in holding that where a child was excluded from the public schools, because in some degree supposed to be an "undesirable citizen," that the parent was compelled to seek its admission in a private or parochial school. There was no presumption that the child, if rejected by the public schools, would be received in a private or parochial school or a school of some other district; therefore, in the last analysis the question of compulsory vaccination came up.

If exclusion for failure to comply with the rule of a public school regarding vaccination was no defense to a prosecution under the compulsory education act, then the exclusion for violation of a similar rule in private or parochial or other district schools would be no defense, and we would then be face to face with a compulsory vaccination law. Besides, the father in this case elected to send his child to a public school, claimed that he did so send the child, and offered to continue to do so. The validity of his conviction must rest upon proof of his sending or failing to send his child to the public schools. The evidence showed that the child was willing to go to school and the parent anxious to have it go. On these facts, the court held that the conviction in a lower court was unlawful, and the judgment of the court of common pleas reversing the conviction and discharging the parent was affirmed.

The New York Case.—In a New York case, a man's son within the compulsory age had been in attendance at a public school and had not been vaccinated.[22] Acting under and in accordance with the provisions of the public health law of the state which provided that "no child or person not vaccinated shall be admitted or received into any of the public schools of the state, and the trustees or other officers having the charge, management, or control of such schools shall cause this provision of law to be enforced," the board of education of the city of New York had passed by-laws providing that no pupil be allowed to attend the public schools unless he had been vaccinated. Under this rule, the child in the case was excluded from the public school. The father was tried in a magistrate's court and convicted of violating the provisions of the compulsory education law. He appealed to the court of general sessions of the peace in the County of New York, where the judgment of the court below was affirmed. He then appealed to the appellate division of the supreme court where the judgment was again affirmed. He finally appealed to the supreme court of the state.

This court in reaffirming the previous judgments argued that a parent should not be allowed to escape his duty to send his child to school, as provided by law, on any excuse which was not an ample justification for such course. The public school system had been developed with great pains and solicitude, and its maintenance and support had been recognized as so important for the welfare of the state that they had been provided for and safeguarded in the constitution itself. As a part of the system, a statute had been passed requiring attendance at school of children within certain limits. If indifferent or selfish parents for ulterior purposes, such as a desire to place young children at labor instead of in school, or from capricious or recalcitrant mo-

[22] People v. Ekerold, 211 N. Y., 386. Decided 1914.

tives, might be allowed to manufacture easy excuses for not sending their children to school, a ready method would have been developed for evading the statute compelling such attendance. If the statute which required parents to see to it that their children attended and took advantage of this school system might be lightly and easily evaded, the purposes of the state in providing and insisting on education would be frustrated and impaired. Failure to comply with the statute ought not to be excused except for some good reason.

The statute and the by-laws of the board of education requiring vaccination as a condition of attending the public schools were not so unusual or oppressive that a parent should be allowed to make his unwillingness to comply therewith a basis for not sending his child to school. The statute requiring vaccination as a condition of attending the public schools was well within the police powers of the state. While it could not be exactly and absolutely demonstrated that vaccination prevented smallpox, and while some authorities disputed this proposition, the prevalent belief was that it did have that effect. Therefore, it was for the legislature in the exercise of its discretion to decide this question and, if it considered that the remedy was effective, to pass such a statute in the interest of public health. It must be assumed that the law requiring vaccination of children in the public schools was a proper one.

The statute requiring vaccination was adopted in 1893, the one requiring attendance upon instruction in 1894. It did not seem reasonable to assume that it was the legislative intention in passing both of these statutes relating to attendance at school to provide and have it come to pass that unwillingness to comply with the one requiring vaccination might be turned into a good excuse for disobeying the other one concerning attendance. It did not require much spirit of prophecy to foresee what would follow a contrary construction of the statutes. If a parent might escape all obligation under the statute requiring him to send his child to school by simply alleging that he did not believe in vaccination, the policy of the state to give some education to all children, if necessary by compelling measures, would become more or less of a farce under existing legislation.

The defendant had the choice of sending his child to a private school or educating it otherwise. The defendant's reply to this suggestion was that that would entail expense. That might or might not be so, and even if it were it would not be sufficient to excuse the present position and situation of the defendant. The government at the present day, in the exercise of its police powers, imposed many regulations which involved trouble and expense, and such trouble and expense had not been regarded as an excuse for noncompliance. If the defendant did not desire to take advantage of the public schools under the conditions prescribed for their operation, it very possibly might result that he would incur some additional trouble in the education of his children elsewhere. The choice rested with him, and the burdens of either would doubtless be fully compensated by the benefits to accrue from furnishing an education to his child. The vaccination statute considered in this case applied only to the public schools.

Another New York Case.—A parent was convicted in a justice court of New York for a violation of the compulsory education law, and appealed to the county court, which affirmed the conviction.[23] A truant officer of the district had laid information before the justice of the peace charging this parent with having committed a misdemeanor in that he failed to cause his two children, who were between the ages of seven and sixteen years, to attend upon instruction as provided by the education law of the state. A warrant was issued, the parent arrested and brought before the justice of the peace. He was tried before the justice and a jury, found guilty as charged, and fined by the justice the sum of five dollars, and in default of payment was to be imprisoned not to exceed five days.

In reviewing the case, the county court stated that prior to the opening of the school, the school trustee had personally notified this parent, and all other parents of the district, that the public health law in relation to vaccination, and the education law in relation to attendance would be enforced in the district. Neither of the children had been vaccinated. After affording the parent a reasonable opportunity to comply with the law, the trustee instructed the teacher to exclude the children from school, and notified them that they could not attend until vaccinated. The children were then absent from school seven days, when this action against the parent was instituted. There was no claim made by the parent, and the evidence conclusively established

[23] People v. McIlwain, 151, N.Y.S. 366. Decided 1915.

the fact that the children did not receive instruction equivalent to that furnished by the school in the district outside of said school.

The attorneys of the parent urged the reversal of judgment of conviction on three grounds:

1. That it appeared by the evidence that this parent did not at any time refuse to send his children to school, but that, on the contrary, he caused them to go to school, and that they had been sent home from school by the teacher, and told that they would not be admitted until they had been vaccinated; that the parent had refused to have his children vaccinated, and was not guilty of having violated the compulsory attendance law.

2. That it appeared by the evidence introduced by the state at the trial that each of the children of this parent was subject to chronic sore throat, pharyngitis, and other throat diseases, and that the parent sought to prove by a duly licensed and practicing physician and surgeon that the vaccination of the children would under these circumstances be liable to result in serious injury to the health of the children, and that the evidence of the physician was excluded against the objection of the counsel for the parent.

3. That the trustee of the school district had not adopted a resolution excluding children and persons not vaccinated from attending school, and did not give the ten days' notice of such resolution as provided by the health law of the state.

The court argued that the fact that this parent sent his children to the schoolhouse some of the days during the period in question was no defense, and did not relieve him from the penalty imposed by the statute. The proceeding was for the purpose of imposing a penalty upon the parent for failure to comply with the requirements of the education law and the public health law. The state, speaking through the legislature, had enacted a requirement that all children between the ages of eight and fourteen years should attend school during the entire time the school in the district was in session. The education law provided that it should be the duty of the parents of such children to cause them to attend upon instruction as required by the law. The public school system was free, and the state in maintaining it and affording all the children an opportunity for an education imposed certain conditions to be complied with to entitle such children to attend. If the conditions were not complied with, the right to enjoy the benefits of the free public schools did not exist, and the parent must furnish equivalent instruction elsewhere.

In this case, the parent did not cause his children to comply with the conditions imposed by the state to entitle them to attend school, did not furnish equivalent instruction elsewhere, but insisted upon his right to send his children to school as he saw fit. This assertion upon his part of a right to exercise his individual judgment did not set the statute aside, and the fact that he sent the children to the schoolhouse was no defense whatever, for he did refuse to send them to school prepared to attend, as the law required, and he did fail and refuse to furnish them opportunity for instruction equivalent to that which they would receive in the school.

Excluding the testimony of the physician was not an error on the part of the justice of the peace. That testimony was offered for the purpose of proving that vaccination was dangerous and the law unjust. If this proceeding had been instituted for the purpose of compelling the parent to vaccinate the children, the evidence of the physician might have been competent; but such was not the purpose of the proceeding. It was a matter of indifference to the people, the truant officer, and the state, whether this parent caused his children to be vaccinated or not, and the question of the effect of vaccination upon these particular children, or in general, was entirely an immaterial matter; therefore, the evidence was incompetent for any purpose in this proceeding. The proceeding was not brought against the parent for failure to cause his children to be vaccinated, but was brought for failure on his part to comply with the requirements for admission into the school, and for failure on his part to satisfy the requirements of the statute by furnishing his children with equivalent instruction elsewhere.

The health law was a positive and mandatory law, and imposed an explicit duty upon school officers by providing that no child not vaccinated should be admitted or received into any public school; and that the officers having charge and control of the school should cause the provision to be enforced. No discretion was vested by this enactment; no exception was made; it was the law of the state to be obeyed by every citizen and to be enforced by every school official enacted by the legislature, and not dependent for life, force, or effect upon the discretion, whim, or caprice of any board of school officials or individual school trustees.

Another Pennsylvania Case.—A Pennsylvania case came up to a district court as an appeal from the judgment of a magistrate in imposing a fine of two dollars and costs in each case of two children for violation of the compulsory education law.[24] The father sent his children to school but they were refused admission because he would not have them vaccinated.

The question for decision in this case was whether the defendant was excused from the imposition of a fine provided by the compulsory attendance law of 1911 for failure to send his child to school, notwithstanding he was willing and endeavored to comply with the act, and his children were excluded by the school authorities unless the children were vaccinated or had previously had smallpox.

The court held that the provisions of the Act of 1911 for attendance at school within required ages were general and mandatory, and the only exceptions permitted from their operation were those specified in the act on account of physical or mental impediment to attendance or study, and even then the exceptions were operative only by excuse from attendance given by the board of school directors of the district upon satisfactory proof of the conditions justifying it.

The object to be attained was the attendance of every child of the prescribed age at school: "Such child or children shall attend such school continuously through the entire term during which the public elementary schools in their respective districts shall be in session." Nothing less than such attendance could work the benefits contemplated by the compulsory education provisions of the law; namely, the teaching of all children of the state in the common English branches; and nothing could be allowed to defeat the accomplishment of those benefits except for reasons specified in the Act. When, therefore, the Act imposed upon all persons having a parental relation the duty of sending a child or children to a school, there was necessarily involved the performance by such person of any concomitant duty required by law as a prerequisite to the attendance at school required in the Act. The legislation of 1911, making it obligatory upon every parent to have his child or children in attendance at school was enacted

[24] Commonwealth v. Gillen, 25 Pa. D.R. 401. Decided 1916.

with the knowledge of the legislators that such attendance could not be had, nor could the duty imposed on parents be performed, unless a certificate of successful vaccination of the child, or of its previously having had smallpox, were presented to the school authorities as required by the Act of 1895. With such knowledge, the legislature imposed upon the parent the absolute duty of having his child or children in school, and made no provision for excuse from such duty by failure or inability of the parent to furnish the certificate required by law as to vaccination. The conclusion seemed irresistible that the legislature contemplated and intended the furnishing of such certificate as incident to and a part of the duty of sending the child to school as imposed by the Act of 1911. The legislature must be taken to have intended that the mandate of compulsory attendance contained in the Act of 1911 should be obeyed and fulfilled in a lawful manner, in compliance with and not in violation of the requirements for attendance imposed by the Act of 1895, and, therefore, that the procurement and production of the certificate provided for in the latter should form a constituent part of the duty of each parent to have and keep his child or children in attendance at school. Therefore, the failure of a parent to procure and produce such certificate and the consequent exclusion of his child from school, could not be used as an excuse for nonperformance of his duty under the Act of 1911 to have and keep his child in attendance at school.

The defendant did not comply with the law in his allegation that "his wife who had had a public school education had been instructing their children." The law required that instruction given outside of school would be a compliance with the Act if given "by a properly qualified private tutor" and "if such instruction is satisfactory to the proper county or district superintendent of schools."

The schools affected by the law of 1895 concerning vaccination included "any public, private, parochial, Sunday, or other school."

Third Pennsylvania Case.—In another Pennsylvania case, a parent had sent a child of compulsory school age to school.[25] She had been refused admission by the principal because she did not produce a certificate of vaccination. Besides, the board of school directors had not excused the child because of any mental, physi-

[25] Commonwealth v. Aiken, 64 Pa. Superior Ct. 96. Decided 1916.

he argument of the court delivered at
ve with that in the preceding case. The
at the Vaccination Act of 1895 and the
ture of the School Code of 1911 should
effect to both, and this might be done,
lling vaccination of the child, but by
ns.

se.—That the Pennsylvania courts will
ry vaccination law and the compulsory
d by another decision in that state.[26]
district were tried in a justice of the
for failure to enforce the vaccination
e county court.

This court decided that the legislature by Act of 1895 imposed a duty on school directors and others to refuse the admittance of unvaccinated children to the schools, and this duty having been imposed, the breach thereof was an offense criminal in its nature, punishable upon conviction before a justice of the peace, and the action was not for the question of a penalty in the nature of an action of debt. It was a proceeding to convict for a violation of the law and it could not be said that the only party interested was the one who received the fine, and that since the Commonwealth was not entitled to the fine, it had no interest.

This decision indicates that the state and the court would not permit school officials to evade the enforcement of the vaccination law, and thereby allow parents to escape the penalties of the compulsory attendance law.

Summary

1. More litigation has reached the courts relative to compulsory attendance and vaccination than to any other classification of this chapter.

2. This controversy has been going on during the first nineteen years of this century, the decisions dating from 1900 to 1919.

3. The principle of the first decision—Pennsylvania, 1900—was that if a parent sent his child to school and the child was refused admittance because he was not vaccinated, the parent could not be punished under the compulsory attendance law nor compelled to provide instruction for his child.

[26] Commonwealth v. Wilkins et. al., 12 Erie, Pa.

4. The principle of the second decision in time—Michigan, 1901—was that in the absence of a state law requiring vaccination, no local board could make a rule excluding unvaccinated children from school, and then proceed against the parents under the compulsory attendance law. Boards might refuse admission to unvaccinated children during the prevalence of smallpox, but the power ceased when the emergency ended. The Missouri and Ohio cases, both in 1909, held to the same principle.

5. The Minnesota decision in 1902 held that the requirements of the public health were primary and superior to the rights and the duty of pupils to attend school, and that even if the legislature did not specifically confer the power on local authorities to require vaccination for school attendance, it intended to do so, and the exercise of such power was permissible. This decision represents a loose construction of the law, whereas the Michigan, Missouri, and Ohio decisions represent strict constructions.

6. By 1909, the Washington decision held that both compulsory vaccination and compulsory attendance were within the power of of the legislature to enact. Requiring successful vaccination as a condition of school membership did not repeal the law requiring compulsory attendance.

7. The decisions of 1914 and 1915 in New York and of 1916 and 1919 in Pennsylvania all support strongly the principles that unvaccinated children must be excluded from public schools and that parents of such children can escape punishment under the compulsory attendance laws only by providing private instruction satisfactory to the school authorities.

PRIVATE AND PAROCHIAL SCHOOL INSTRUCTION

The number of decisions in which the legality of attendance on private or parochial school instruction was an issue indicates considerable controversy over this matter. The sources gave seven decisions in seven different states, ranking in time from 1893 to 1925. The states and the year of the decision in each are:

Massachusetts	1893
Indiana	1904
Pennsylvania	1906
Washington	1912
Kansas	1916
Oklahoma	1922
Oregon	1924 and 1925

The Massachusetts Case.—In Massachusetts, the charge was made against a parent that he kept his child of compulsory school age out of the public school the required length of time for attendance; that he did not have her attend a private school approved by the school committee for an equal period of time; that he did not have her otherwise instructed for a like period of time in the branches of learning required by law to be taught in the public schools; and that his child's physical and mental condition was not such as to render such attendance inexpedient or impracticable.[27]

The parent offered to show that for a like period of time alleged in the complaint, and during the time alleged, his child had been instructed in the branches of learning required by law to be taught in the public schools in a private day school not approved by the school committee; that application to approve said private school had been made to the school committee and refused. The judge of the superior court refused to admit this evidence, or to rule that the facts, if proved, came within the exceptions mentioned in the statute. Under this ruling, the jury returned a verdict of guilty.

An appeal was made to the supreme court of the state. Here the court held that if a parent, instead of sending his child to a public school or to a private day school approved by the school committee, preferred to have him instructed otherwise, it was incumbent on the parent, in order to escape the penalty imposed by the compulsory attendance law, to show that the child had been instructed for the specified period in the required branches of learning, unless the child had already acquired them; and on a complaint alleging the violation of the provisions of the law, the parent might show that for a like period of time with the period alleged in the complaint, and during the time alleged in the complaint, the child had been instructed in a private day school not approved by the school committee in the branches of learning required by law to be taught in the public schools.

In support of this view, the court argued that the great object of the law was that all children should be educated, not that they should be educated in any particular way. To this end, public schools were established so that all children might be sent to them, unless other sufficient means of education were provided for

[27] Commonwealth v. Roberts, 159 Mass. 372. Decided 1893.

them. If the child had in any manner already acquired the branches of learning required by law to be taught in the public schools, the law did not compel any further instruction. If he had not acquired them, the law required that he be instructed in them for the specified time each year. Sending the child to a private day school approved by the committee was enough to comply with the requirements of the law without further inquiry. But if the parent, instead of sending his child to a public school or to a private day school approved by the school committee, preferred to have him instructed otherwise, it would be incumbent on him to show that the child had been instructed for the specified period in the required branches of learning, unless he had already acquired them. This permitted instruction in those branches in schools or academies situated in the same city or town, or elsewhere, or instruction by a private tutor or governess, or by the parents themselves, provided it was given in good faith and was sufficient in extent. If a school committee had not approved of a particular school, or had expressly refused to approve of it, then the parent, if he sent the child to that school, must take the responsibility of being able to prove that he had been sufficiently and properly instructed there. He had no such responsibility if he sent the child to a private day school approved by the school committee.

The court held that the evidence which was excluded in the superior court should have been admitted; and the verdict of that court was set aside.

The Indiana Case.—Eleven years later, a similar case was tried in Indiana.[28] A parent was prosecuted in the circuit court for an alleged violation of the compulsory education law. He was acquitted, and the state appealed to the appellate court.

The parent in good faith had secured the services of a teacher formerly employed in the public schools to teach his child. It was arranged that the child should be taught all the branches taught in the public schools at the regular public school hours. The child attended the teacher's house regularly every school day, and received instruction equal to that which could have been received at the public schools. The teacher did not advertise herself as keeping a private school, and had no regular tuition fixed, nor any school equipment, and made no arrangement to

[28] State v. Peterman, 32 Ind. App. 665. Decided 1904.

take other pupils. Under these conditions, the appellate court held that the parent had complied with the law, which provided that every parent should be required to send his child to a public, private, or parochial school each school year for a term not less than that of the public schools where the child resided.

The court stated that the whole question in the case was: What is a private school within the meaning of the statute? The state had contended for the following instruction, which was refused by the lower court: That a private school within the meaning of the law under which this prosecution was conducted meant a reputable private school organized and conducted as such in good faith by a reputable person or persons, who possess the necessary qualifications as teacher or teachers, and who have the proper equipment for conducting such a school, and who hold themselves out as conducting such a school.

The appellate court said that the instruction was properly refused because it was radically wrong. A school in the ordinary acceptation of its meaning was a place where instruction was imparted to the young. If a parent employed and brought into his residence a teacher for the purpose of instructing his child or children, and such instruction was given as the law contemplated, the meaning and spirit of the law had been fully complied with. This would be the school of the child or children so educated, and would be as much a private school as if advertised and conducted as such. The number of persons, whether one or many, did not make a place where instruction was imparted any less or more a school.

Other instructions tendered by the state were wrong and tainted with the general proposition which pervaded the state's argument to the effect that the law had to do with the way or place where a child should be educated. The purpose of the legislature in taking control of the child, under certain circumstances at a certain period of its life, was to secure to it the opportunity to acquire an education which the welfare of the child and the best interests of society demanded. The result to be obtained, and not the means or manner of obtaining it, was the goal which the lawmakers were attempting to reach. The law was made for the parent who did not educate his child, and not for the parent who employed a teacher and paid him out of his private purse, and so placed within the reach of the child the opportunity and means of acquiring an education equal to that obtainable in the public schools of the state.

The Pennsylvania Case.—The Pennsylvania case came to the district court as an appeal from a conviction of a parent for a violation of the compulsory education law before a justice of the peace.[29] The parent lived within two miles of a public school. He had four children of compulsory school age. Prior to September, 1905, these children attended the public schools of the borough, where the eldest received instruction in reading, writing, spelling, arithmetic, geography, grammar, and physiology. The second child received instruction in the same branches, except geography. What the two younger children were taught did not appear.

Subsequent to September, 1905, this parent sent his four children to a private Polish school in which the only teachers were a father and his son. The latter held no teacher's certificate, and was a boy between fifteen and sixteen years of age. The father taught only in the Polish language. The only instruction in English was by the boy on three days in the week. The only branches taught in the English language were reading and arithmetic, and the only textbooks in English were a primer and a beginner's arithmetic.

The parent was convicted of a violation of the law in that he did not send his children "to a day school in which the common English branches are taught" as required by the state law. The district court held that whether the conviction in the justice court should stand depended upon what construction was to be given to the phrase quoted above as it was used in the law. It was the opinion of the court that the teaching in the Polish school did not meet the requirements of the legislature, and that the defendant was properly convicted by the justice of the peace.

The Washington Case.—The question as to what kind of private instruction fulfilled the requirements of the compulsory education law was before the court in the Washington case.[30] The court held that it was not a compliance with the statute for a parent to give his children of school age private instructions without providing a regular private school for them, which in curriculum and hours was similar to the public schools.

[29] Commonwealth v. Snyder, 15 Pa. D. R. 765. Decided 1906.
[30] State v. Connort, 69 Wash. 361. Decided 1912.

The court argued that a private school might undoubtedly be maintained in a private home in which the children of the instructor might be pupils. The provision of the law was not to be determined by the place where the school was maintained, nor the individuality or number of the pupils who attended it. It was to be determined by the purpose, intent, and character of the endeavor. The evidence of the state in this case was to the effect that the parent concerned maintained no school at his home; that his two little girls could be seen playing about the house at all times during the ordinary school hours. No effort was made to refute this testimony. The parent seemed to be impressed with the belief that if he was a competent and qualified teacher, and gave instruction to his children at his home, he maintained a private school within the meaning of the law. But such was not a compliance with the law.

The Kansas Case.—In the Kansas case, the court held that a parent who took his child out of the public school and sent it regularly to a private, denominational, or parochial school for such period as it was in session was not subject to the penalties of the truancy law.[31] This case came to the supreme court on appeal by the state from a decision in a lower court. The facts, as presented by the state, were that the parent of a child of compulsory age took him out of the public school in April, 1916, while it was still in session, and placed him in a private school taught by a competent instructor, which school was taught in the German language; thereby, according to the state, the child became and was irregular in attendance at school, and was absent from school three or more consecutive days, and thereby became habitually truant from school.

The contention of the state was that a private school, in order to be recognized as a private school and to come within the contemplation of the statute, must be equal in all respects to a public school and must comply with all the statutory requirements prescribed for public schools; that the intent of the legislature in creating public schools and authorizing private, parochial, or denominational schools was to make education compulsory to the degree specified by law.

The court stated that the requirements of the law in regard to private, denominational, or parochial schools was that they must

[31] State v. Will, 99 Kans. 167. Decided 1916.

be taught "by a competent instructor each school year for such period as said school is in session." The court conceded that the argument of the state was supported by some most respectable authorities. But it virtually asked the court to rewrite into the present statute language which the legislature struck out when it revised the law in 1903, and that the court could not do. If the conclusion that the court reached disclosed a defect in the law which was of serious consequences to the educational work of the state, the remedy lay with the legislature. Since the legislature had refrained from exercising control over the courses of study in the private, denominational, or parochial schools further than to require them to be taught by competent instructors, it was too much to ask the state's prosecuting officers or its courts to meddle with them.

The Oklahoma Case.—A parent was convicted in a county court in Oklahoma of violating the compulsory school laws.[32] He appealed to the criminal court of appeals, where the decision of the county court was reversed. The law under which he was convicted provided that it was unlawful for any parent to neglect or refuse to cause his child or children to attend some public or private school, or other school, unless other means of education were provided for a period of two-thirds of the time the public school in the district of his residence was in session.

The mother of the child in the case testified that her daughter was eight years of age; that she, the mother, had given the child instruction in the branches taught in the public school for a period of about five hours each day. The mother was a graduate of a normal training school in which the curriculum included pedagogy, language, literature, history, mathematics, and other branches. She testified that the child was proficient, and offered exhibits of the child's work. The evidence showed that the father was also an expert teacher, having taught a number of years in several different states. He assisted his wife in giving the child instruction. The parents offered to demonstrate in court that the child had received efficient educational training, but the offer was refused.

The court stated that this was ostensibly an action to punish a parent for neglecting the education of his child; in reality the record indicated that the prosecution grew out of religious differ-

[32] Wright v. State, 209 Pacific 179. Decided 1922.

ences and disputes arising out of the management of school affairs, involving a bond issue, the location of a consolidated school building, and methods of instruction and school discipline. The parents were members of the religious sect known as Seventh-day Adventists, and testified that they were desirous of training their children to become missionaries and ministers, and claimed that the training and moral influences in the public school there were not favorable to that end. For this and other reasons, they decided to give this child instruction at home in lieu of a public school training. The court held that so long as the child's education was not neglected, the parents had a right, under the constitution and laws of the state, to manage and supervise the education of their child if done in a fitting and proficient manner. The proof was not at all convincing that the education of this child was being in any way neglected. It seemed to the court that the state, as prosecutors in the case, misunderstood the scope and spirit of the statute upon which this prosecution was heard.

The county court had instructed the jury in part as follows:

> In case a parent neglects to furnish other means of education, it is his duty under the law to furnish the necessary equipment for said child and an instructor, competent to instruct his child in the prescribed course of study as laid down by the state, or in some other course of instruction equal to or better than the course of instruction as laid down by the state, so that the child may be educated to fill its station in life when it reaches its majority.
>
> You are instructed that the state reserves the right to fix the number of hours the children in the state shall be taught, and in that respect you are instructed that a school month shall consist of four weeks of five days each, of six hours per day.
>
> You are instructed that under the laws of the state of Oklahoma no person or persons are authorized or permitted to issue any special permit, certificate, or temporary certificate to any person, authorizing them to teach, except the County Superintendent of the County in which the special permit, certificate, or temporary certificate is to be used, and that in that event such temporary certificate, permit, or special certificate shall only remain in effect until the next regular teacher's examination, and this applies to public schools of the County.

In addition to the foregoing, the county court gave a lengthy instruction defining the qualifications of teachers in public schools. This, the higher court said, the jury might have applied by inference to private tutors. These instructions, the higher court held, were erroneous. Under the terms of the statute, and under the constitution, a parent might have his child instructed by a competent private tutor or educated in a sectarian or other accredited school without a strict adherence to the standard fixed for teachers in the public schools of the state. The statute made no provisions fixing the qualifications of private teachers or teachers in private schools or academies, or to prescribe definite courses of study in such cases. If such schools of instruction were manifestly inadequate, or such instruction were furnished for the sole purpose of evading the proper education of a child, the statute could then be properly invoked. Whether such independent facilities for education, outside of the public schools, were supplied in good faith, or whether they were equivalent to those offered by the state, was a question of fact for the jury, and not a question of law for the court.

The Oregon Case.—The most recent of these cases is the one generally known as the Oregon School case. There are two decisions in this case. The first was rendered by the United States district court of Oregon;[33] the second by the United States supreme court. In 1923, the legislature of Oregon passed a law requiring children of the compulsory school age to attend public schools. The district court held that this law was not valid as an exercise of the police power of the state.

In its argument, the court stated that it was not denied that the state in its sovereign capacity was entitled to the exercise of what are termed police powers. What these powers were the courts had not attempted to define precisely. But, without question, they related to the safety, health, morals, and general welfare of the public. There was, however, a limit to the manner in which these powers might be exercised by the state. They could not be exercised arbitrarily and despotically, nor unless there existed a reasonable relation between the character of the legislation and the policy to be subserved. Nor was the state legislature the final judge of the limitations of the police power. Its enactments might be set aside when found to be unwarranted and arbitrary interference with rights protected by the constitution in carrying on a lawful business or occupation in the use and enjoyment of property. In other words, the exercise of police power was subject to judicial review, and property rights could not be ruthlessly destroyed by wrongful enactment.

[33] Society of Sisters v. Pierce, 296 Federal 928. Decided 1924.

No one questioned the proposition that our public schools were subject to a reasonable supervision by the state through its legislature in the exercise of its police powers for safeguarding the health, morals, and general weal of the public. Nor was it disputed that, while parents possessed a natural and inherent right to the nurture, control, and tutorship of their offspring, they might be brought up according to the parents' conception of what is right and just, decent and respectable, and manly and noble in life, the state yet stood in the position of *parens patriae,* and might exercise its just powers in preparing the child, in future life, to support itself, to serve the state, and in all the relations and duties of adult life to perform well and capably its part.

The real test of this case was: Has the state, through its legislative functions, the power, under the guise of police regulation, to deprive parochial and private school organizations of the liberty and right to carry on their schools for teaching in the grammar grades? The act could not be more effective for utterly destroying the business and occupation of complainants' schools, except perhaps the college and higher preparatory grades, if it had been entitled: "An act to prevent parochial and private schools from teaching the grammar grades." This view served to emphasize the seriousness of the controversy. Indeed, the simile was no stronger than the argument for the adoption of the measure put it: "A divided school can no more succeed than a divided nation!" That such was the purpose of the Act was obvious and incontrovertible.

Compulsory education being the paramount policy of the state, it could not be said with reason and justice that the right and privilege of parochial and private schools to teach in the common school grades was inimical or detrimental to, or destructive of, that policy. The act in question was neither necessary nor essential for the proper enforcement of the state's policy. The melting-pot idea, applied to the common schools of the state, as an incentive for the adoption of the act, was an extravagance in simile.

The complainants in the case contended that they could not maintain their schools, if their patronage was taken away by making it unlawful for parents and guardians to send their children to complainants' schools. The right to carry on their schools, whether parochial or private, was, the court said, a property right, and the right of parents and guardians to send their children and wards to such schools as they might desire, if not in conflict with lawful requirements, was a privilege they inherently were entitled to enjoy.

The state raised the issue that this suit had been prematurely brought; that the act complained against did not become effective until on and after the first day of September, 1926, more than two years and five months later. In reply, the court pointed out that in the very nature of the upbuilding and maintenance of parochial and private schools, when the attendance, prospective as well as required, was taken away or rendered unlawful, it would destroy the pursuit or occupation. If school buildings had been constructed, and equipment purchased and provided, without school attendance, such property must lapse into disuse, and become of no value for the purposes for which it was designed. An irreparable loss would ensue—the paramount loss of school attendance, and a damage and practical destruction, especially for school purposes, of the school property. The work of destruction had already set in. The complainants were losing their patronage, traceable directly to the fact that the act was a statute, duly adopted and promulgated. Parents were looking to the future, and were laying their plans to meet the exigencies to arise. The curriculum of the grade schools required several years of attendance, and if parents must, on the taking effect of the statute, send their children to the public schools, many of them were prepared to do so now or as convenience might suggest. Hence the drawing away of complainants' patronage had set in, and would continue with increased progression until the day when all would be lost.

It was the opinion of the court that the state, acting in its legislative capacity, had, in the means adopted, exceeded the limitations of its power—its purpose being to take utterly away from complainants their constitutional right and privilege to teach in the grammar grades—and had deprived and would deprive them of their property without due process of law.

The state of Oregon appealed from this decision to the United States supreme court.[34] This court stated that the manifest purpose of the law which was being contested was to compel general attendance at public schools by normal children between eight

[34] Pierce v. Society of Sisters, 268 U.S. 510. Decided 1925.

and sixteen, who had not completed the eighth grade. Enforcement of the statute would seriously impair, perhaps destroy, the profitable features of the Society's business and greatly diminish the value of its property.

The district court had ruled that the Fourteenth Amendment guaranteed the Society against the deprivation of its property without due process of law consequent upon the unlawful interference by the state with the free choice of patrons, present and prospective. It declared that the right to conduct schools was property and that parents and guardians as a part of their liberty might direct the education of children by selecting reputable teachers and places. It declared, too, that these schools were not unfit or harmful to the public, and that enforcement of the challenged statute would unlawfully deprive them of patronage, and thereby destroy their owners' business and property. Finally, that the threats to enforce the act would continue to cause irreparable injury, and the suits were not premature.

No question was raised, argued the supreme court, concerning the power of the state reasonably to regulate all schools, to inspect, supervise, and examine them, their teachers, and pupils; to require that all children of proper age attend some school, that teachers should be of good moral character and patriotic disposition, that certain studies plainly essential to good citizenship must be taught, and that nothing be taught which was manifestly inimical to the public welfare.

The inevitable result of enforcing the Act would be destruction of the Society's primary schools, and perhaps all other private primary schools for normal children in the state of Oregon. The Society was engaged in an undertaking not inherently harmful, but long regarded as useful and meritorious. There was nothing in the present records to indicate that the Society had failed to discharge obligations to patrons, students, or the state. And there were no peculiar circumstances or present emergencies which demanded extraordinary measures relative to primary education.

It was entirely plain that the Act of 1922 unreasonably interfered with the liberty of parents and guardians to direct the upbringing and education of children under their control. Rights guaranteed by the constitution might not be abridged by legislation which had no reasonable relation to some purpose within the competency of the state. The fundamental theory of liberty upon which all governments in this Union reposed excluded any general power of the state to standardize its children by forcing them to accept instruction from public teachers only. The child was not the mere creature of the state; those who nurtured him and directed his destiny had the right, coupled with the high duty, to recognize and prepare him for additional obligations.

The Society was a corporation, and therefore, it was said, the members could not claim for themselves the liberty which the Fourteenth Amendment guaranteed. Accepted in the proper sense, this was true. But they had business and property for which they claimed protection. These were threatened with destruction through the unwarranted compulsion which the state was exercising over present and prospective patrons of their schools. The supreme court had gone very far to protect against loss threatened by such action.

Generally it was entirely true, as urged by counsel for the state, that no person in any business had such an interest in possible customers as to enable him to restrain exercise of proper power of the state upon the ground that he would be deprived of patronage. But the injunctions sought were not against the exercise of any proper power. The Society asked protection against arbitrary, unreasonable, and unlawful interference with its patrons and the consequent destruction of its business and property. Its interest was clear and immediate with the rule approved in many cases where injunctions had issued to protect business enterprises against interference with the freedom of patrons or customers.

The suits were not premature. The injury to the Society was present and very real, not a mere possibility in the remote future. If no relief had been possible prior to the effective date of the Act, the injury would have become irreparable. Prevention of impending injury by unlawful action was a well-recognized function of courts of equity.

Summary

1. Private and parochial school instruction are upheld by the courts. Tests as to the proficiency of pupils under this instruction are suggested in the Massachusetts, Oklahoma, and Indiana cases.

2. In the Washington and Indiana decisions, the standards are

set up that private instruction include the regular branches of the public schools taught during the regular hours of such schools.

3. In the Pennsylvania decision, private school instruction given mostly in the Polish language was not lawful; in the Kansas decision private instruction given entirely in the German language was lawful.

4. Private instruction, in the opinion of the courts, does not have to be given in a particular way, nor does it have to meet the strict requirements of the public schools as to qualifications of teachers, equipment, and course of study. The purpose, intent, and character of the endeavor are to be taken into account in determining the sufficiency of the instruction.

5. Legislation requiring children of the compulsory age to attend only public schools is unconstitutional.

6. The power of states reasonably to regulate private and parochial instruction is not questioned by the courts.

CONSTRUING THE LAW AS TO AGE LIMITS

The Michigan Case.—In the enforcement of compulsory attendance requirements, the courts have been resorted to for constructions as to age limits. A case of this kind arose in Michigan over a conflict between a prosecuting attorney and the judge of a recorder's court.[35] The attorney requested the judge to issue a warrant for a parent for violation of the compulsory education law, which required parents of "children between and including the ages of seven and fifteen years to send such children to the public schools during the entire school year." The child in this case was fifteen years and three months of age. The recorder refused to issue a warrant, for the reason that in his opinion the law had not been violated. The circuit court gave an order to show why a writ of mandamus should not be issued compelling the recorder to prepare said warrant, and upon a hearing the writ was denied, and the proceeding dismissed. The prosecuting attorney then took action to have the case heard in the supreme court.

Six justices of the court concurred in a prevailing opinion, and two gave a dissenting opinion. The decision was an interpretation of what was "the intent of the legislature." The words before the court for construction were: "any child or children

[35] Jackson v. Mason, 145 Mich. 338. Decided 1906.

between and including the ages of seven and fifteen years." The prosecutor urged that to give any force to the word "including," the section must be construed to include children during the entire fifteenth year and until they become sixteen years old. The court held this to be a doubtful construction and would hesitate to make an act a crime by such means. The statute was not ambiguous in designating the age limit between the ages of seven and fifteen years. The word, including, had no force to extend that limit beyond the time specifically designated. A child over fifteen years of age was not between the ages of seven and fifteen, and therefore not within the provisions of this act. The judgment of the circuit court was affirmed.

The opinion of the dissenting judges was that the statute treated the year as the unit, and that it followed that the words "seven to fifteen years inclusive" included the year in which the child was generally spoken of as fifteen years of age.

The Texas Case.—In a Texas case, the court had to construe the age limit in the law which provided that every child of eight and not more than fourteen years old shall be required to attend public schools, etc.[36] The court held the law was not applicable to a child whose fourteenth birthday came October 12th, and the school term in the district of his residence did not begin until October 30th.

The court argued that it was obvious that the general assembly intended to fix some limit to the age of children affected by the statute—a point of time beyond which they no longer were amenable to its provisions. In one sense, a child was sixteen years of age until it was seventeen; so also it was sixteen when it was eighteen. But, in the true sense, it was sixteen and over whenever it had passed beyond the first day of the sixteenth anniversary of its birth. Had it been the intention to include children up to the time they reached their seventeenth birthday, the general assembly would naturally have said "children under seventeen years of age."

The Tennessee Case.—A parent in a Tennessee case was convicted in a circuit court of a failure to comply with the compulsory education statute.[37] He appealed to the supreme court, charging error. The circuit court held that the words in the law,

[36] Butler v. State, 194 S. W. 166. Decided 1917.
[37] Covell v. State, 227 S. W. 41. Decided 1921.

"between the ages of seven and sixteen years, inclusive," required that a child of sixteen years and six months be sent to school.

In its argument, the supreme court stated that no justification was offered by the parent for keeping his child out of school, save that the proper construction of the statute excluded a child who had passed its sixteenth birthday. The court thought that the language used in the statute to fix the ages was entirely free from ambiguity, and that no extended discussion of statutory construction was required to arrive at the intention of the legislature. The words were to be taken in their usual and ordinary acceptation, and, so considered, must apply to children in their seventh, sixteenth, and intermediate years, as these respective ages were customarily referred to. It was technically true that one reached a particular age at a fixed or certain point of time, but, having attained the designated birthday, one's age, as ordinarily alluded to, continued as of the latter birthday until the succeeding one was reached. Literally speaking, one was of the exact age of twenty-one years for only one day, but in common acceptance one's age was spoken of as twenty-one until the arrival of the twenty-second birthday—the year, and not the day being the unit of measurement. The decision of the lower court was affirmed.

Summary

1. Three statements as to age limits were construed in these decisions, as follows:

   A. Between and including the ages of seven and fifteen years.
   B. Children of eight years and not more than fourteen years of age.
   C. Between the ages of seven and sixteen years inclusive.

2. In the case of (A) the court construed the upper limit to be the fifteenth birthday. In the case of (C) the court construed the upper limit to be the seventeenth birthday. These apparently conflicting decisions, and the necessity for decisions at all, indicate how confusing this matter of determining the compulsory age limits must be. The arguments of the courts show that the only definite way of fixing age limits that do not need to be interpreted is by the use of birthdays. For example, from the seventh birthday to the fifteenth birthday is understood by every one, and a legislature using such language would not have to have its

intention determined or language construed by the courts. Yet in the case of only one state, Virginia, is the statement of the age limits made in such language as to preclude the necessity of construction. The Virginia law uses the language "reached the eighth birthday and not past the fourteenth."

3. The language fixing the age limits in the compulsory education laws of the states may be classified under six types as follows

A. Expressions like "between 8 and 16" .... 30 states
B. Expressions like "between 7 and 15 inclusive" .... 7 states
C. Expressions like "over 7 and under 16" .... 5 states
D. Expressions like "not less than 7 nor more than 14" .... 4 states
E. Expressions like "7 to 16" .... 2 states
F. Expressions like "reached 8th birthday and not past 14th" ...... 1 state

One state, Maryland, uses two of these types of statement; one for city schools, the other for rural.

EXTENSION OF SCHOOL ATTENDANCE PERIOD

Legislation that has extended the period of compulsory attendance has required interpretation and application in the courts. A parent had been convicted in a justice of the peace court in Pennsylvania for keeping his boy out of school in violation of the compulsory education law.[38] He appealed to a higher court. The boy at the time of prosecution was about fifteen and one-half years of age. He had completed the grammar school course, and had received a certificate to that effect which entitled him to admission to high school. He was physically and mentally sound, but was not attending any school in the district. Notice had been served on the father to appear before the school board and show cause why this boy should not be sent to school as required by law, but the notice was ignored. The boy did not hold an employment certificate of any kind.

The court stated that in the absence of any evidence that the boy was regularly engaged in some useful employment or service during the time the public schools were in session, or that he held an employment certificate, issued according to law, the admitted facts in the case were decisive against the father, and the judgment of the justice of the peace should be affirmed. The father did not avail himself of the one defense which would have been a full and unanswerable one in the case, and that was having

[38] Commonwealth v. Levey, 22 Pa. D. R. 285. Decided 1912.

an employment certificate. The counsel for the father claimed that there was a distinction between a public elementary school in which only the common branches were taught, and a public high school, and that the law made no provision for compulsory attendance of the high school. The court replied that if it had been the intention of the legislature to excuse from further attendance all pupils who had satisfactorily completed the course of study prescribed for the eighth grade or grammar department of the public schools, regardless of the age of the pupil at that time, the act would have expressed that intention in clear and unequivocal language. This it had not done but had expressly stated what should be considered compliance with the provisions pertaining to compulsory attendance, and what should be a sufficient excuse for noncompliance.

The court did not agree with the view that a certificate of graduation from the eighth grade, entitling entrance to high school, exempted a pupil from further attendance at the public schools of his district. To hold so would nullify the plain terms of an important act of the assembly. It might be, as argued by counsel for the defendant, that a common school education alone was compulsory under the school code. But, if so, the assembly had provided that all children between the ages of eight and sixteen years must regularly attend the public school continuously through the entire term during which the schools should be in session, unless nonattendance was excused in accordance with the provisions of the law.

Some children were more apt than others and more advanced at ten or twelve than others at sixteen, and many pupils would not have secured a common school education by sixteen. To hold that the intention of the act was to compel the pupil to acquire a common school education would be to make school attendance uncertain and indefinite, and might well result in compelling some pupils to attend school from the time they became of school age until their majority; while some prodigies might complete the course when but twelve or fourteen years of age. Such a construction would surround the whole matter of compulsory attendance with doubt and uncertainty.

The purpose for the compulsory attendance of pupils was twofold: first, the education of the pupil in the common English branches at least; second, the subjection of pupils to proper training and discipline during what might well be called the formation period in the development of character. To be excused from attendance, a pupil between the ages of fourteen and sixteen must be able to read and write intelligently, must be engaged in some useful and lawful employment of service during the time the public schools were in session, and must hold an employment certificate issued according to law.

The court should construe the provisions of the act in a reasonable manner and so as to accomplish the general purposes intended by the framers thereof, and should not, except in cases of an absolute necessity, adopt a construction that would defeat or impair any of its provisions. To construe the provisions as to compulsory attendance in strict conformity with the express terms of the act would not impose any hardship upon any parent or person in parental relation having control or charge of any child or children. These provisions at most required of such a person the performance of duties that ought to be considered binding upon him without any act of assembly. The neglect of some of such persons to perform these duties led to this and similar acts of assembly; and the best interests of the parent, the child, and the commonwealth required that such provisions be enforced against all persons who neglected to comply therewith.

The counsel for the defendant contended that the certificate of graduation issued to the boy entitled him to an employment certificate had he applied for it, hence all conditions of the law had been complied with except obtaining the certificate. It might be conceded, replied the court, that the certificate of graduation was satisfactory evidence of his ability to read and write intelligently, but it did not even tend to show that he was regularly engaged in any useful and lawful employment or service during the time public schools were in session; nor was there any evidence, in the absence of an employment certificate, to show what the nature and extent of the alleged, or rather assumed, employment was. And in addition to the employment mentioned in the law, the language of the act was "and who holds an employment certificate issued according to law."

Furthermore, it would be a violation of law for any person to employ said boy, unless he had an employment certificate issued to him according to law. Hence it would be a most unusual construction of the law to hold that the employment of a boy between the ages of fourteen and sixteen years, who held no employment certificate as required by law, would under the law be a defense to a prosecution against a parent for neglecting to send his boy to school as required by law.

The act of the assembly known as the School Code was presumed to represent the latest and most advanced thought of the people of the state on the question of public schools. It was passed for the betterment of the public school system with a view to promoting the best interests, not only of parents and children, but of society and the commonwealth as well. Courts should, therefore, so construe the act as to give it full force and effect wherever possible, rather than to nullify it by mere technical construction. The judgment of the justice of the peace was affirmed.

The Wisconsin Case.—A case involving continuation school attendance came up in Wisconsin.[39] It was an appeal to the supreme court from a decision of the juvenile court of Milwaukee County. The appellant was charged before the juvenile court, December 6, 1916, with being a delinquent girl of the age of sixteen years, because of her having unlawfully failed, neglected, and refused to attend continuation school as required by law. The case was tried on a plea of not guilty. The appellant was sixteen years of age September 13, 1916. She resided in a city where a continuation school was established. She was a graduate of a grammar school, had taken one year's study in high school, and was a graduate of a business college. From March, 1916, to the commencement of the action, she was employed by a publisher in the city of Milwaukee, and her place of employment was seven miles from her home. She worked first as a stenographer, and then as a bookkeeper. She attended the continuation school Tuesday afternoons for two months prior to the time in November when she ceased working as a stenographer. Thereafter, her employment as a bookkeeper so occupied her time that she could not, and her employer would not allow her to, attend school. She was willing to attend continuation school Saturday afternoons in the city of Milwaukee, and Hoffman Business College therein between 9 and 10 o'clock A. M. for the purpose of obtaining instruction in penmanship, which she needed and could not obtain in the continuation school in her home city. She was a good stu-

[39] State v. Freudenberg, 163 N. W. 184. Decided 1917.

dent and was quite accomplished for one of her years and station. She neglected and refused to attend the continuation school in said city after she was employed as bookkeeper, though she and her parents were notified of the law requiring her to do so. She was willing to obey the law in the future. The juvenile court refused to discharge her, and held that she was a delinquent as charged, but granted a stay of enforcement of the decision pending an appeal to the supreme court, which was taken.

The supreme court stated that the legislature had provided that a minor between the ages of sixteen and seventeen years, in the circumstances mentioned in the statute, should attend continuation school as therein provided. The idea seemed to be that a minor, during the sixteenth year, should not take or be offered employment away from home so as to preclude attending school as the statute provided; that if not in such employment there would be no reason why such attendance should not occur.

The statute required continuous attendance for the prescribed number of hours per week in six consecutive months. While the record was not very clear in respect to the matter, it seemed that the trial court considered that, subsequent to the commencement of the action, there was not time for the appellant to attend the school for the requisite continuous period during the balance of the school year spanned by her sixteenth year, and that she habitually neglected and refused to attend after she had attended for about two months. She, therefore, violated the law before the action was commenced, both in respect to such period of attendance and in being habitually truant.

Much of the evidence in the trial which was offered on behalf of the appellant was to show that she had such educational qualifications that she was not a proper subject for continuation school training, and that under the circumstances it was greatly to her advantage to forego such training, pursue her vocation as a bookkeeper, and take advantage of the facilities offered her for such instruction as would be of use to her in such business. A strong case was made in that regard. Probably in the particular instance it was to the advantage of the minor to lose the continuation school training and retain her place as an employee, rather than to lose the latter in order to have the benefit of the former. But that did not seem to be a legal excuse for her conduct. The statute was mandatory, requiring girls circumstanced as she was to attend continuation school or remain out of employment. It did not seem to admit of any exception. It was one of the numerous child labor laws which the legislature had seen fit to place on the statute books for the purpose of promoting the welfare of minors and preparing them for adult activities. Some of such laws might seem rather extreme regulations. Doubtless, a strict enforcement in some instances might be harmful, but courts must take the law as the legislature made it so long as it was within constitutional limitations. They could not make exceptions thereto to fit particular situations. To do so was within legislative authority; with the lawmaking power rested the sole responsibility for restrictive but constitutional enactments.

The decision appealed from was affirmed, and the cause remanded for further proceedings according to law.

The Indiana Case.—A parent in Indiana was tried and acquitted in the circuit court on a charge of violating the compulsory attendance law.[40] The state appealed to the supreme court.

In the school year 1914-15, the daughter, then twelve years of age, attended the district school and was regularly graduated therefrom in the spring of 1915, after having completed the full prescribed course of study ending with the eighth grade. During the following year she attended no public, private, or parochial day school of any character—although a public high school was maintained within three miles of the parent's residence—but pursued the study of music under private teachers, taking one lesson a week and studying at home for two hours a day. The prosecution on which this appeal was based proceeded on the theory that the parent, in failing to send his child to a school of general instruction during the year 1915-16, violated the provisions of the statute which required children between the ages of seven and fourteen inclusive to attend school regularly, and he accordingly became subject to the penalty of the law.

The parent contended, and the circuit court held, that as his child had satisfactorily completed the study of such branches as are required by law to be taught in the grade schools, the purpose of the statute had been fulfilled, and she could not be compelled to receive any further instruction. This assertion rested in part on the false premise that the term "common schools," as used in the statute, had reference only to the grade or elementary

[40] State v. O'Dell, 118 N. E. 529. Decided 1918.

schools, whereas, by express statutory definition the phrase, which was synonymous with "public schools," was made to include high schools as well. Furthermore, the compulsory education law did not assume to define the several branches of learning in which a child should receive instruction. The legislature, in the exercise of undoubted authority, had determined that individual interest, as well as the good of the future citizenship of the state, required that between the ages of seven and sixteen inclusive every child who was qualified and who was not lawfully employed after reaching the age of fourteen should pursue a study of the general branches of learning. Ample provision was made for a course of study which should cover that period, and sufficient opportunity remained thereafter for the development of individual ambition.

The appeal of the state against the judgment of acquittal in the circuit court was sustained.

Another Indiana Case.—In another Indiana case, a parent was convicted of a violation of the school attendance act in a juvenile court of a county.[41] He appealed to the appellate court of the state where the judgment below was affirmed.

The public high school of the township in which this parent and his child resided was not located in the elementary school district of their residence. On the basis of this fact, the father claimed to be exempt from the application of the law in so far as the attendance of his child at high school was concerned. The court held that the law did not sustain this claim. Township trustees, under certain conditions, were authorized to establish and maintain high schools, and the schools when so established and maintained were a part of the public school system. From a consideration of the law, it was clear that when such high school was established, the entire township became the school district which it was to serve. It was therefore coextensive with all the elementary school districts of the township.

When the school attendance act of 1921 provided that "such child shall attend such school each year during the entire time the public schools are in session in the school district in which such child resides," it did not refer to elementary school districts alone, but to such children who are within the age limit prescribed, between seven and sixteen, and have been graduated from the elementary schools of such township. The entire township was the

[41] Miller v. State, 134 N. E. 209. Decided 1922.

school district intended, wherein a public high school had been established and was being maintained. The course of study to be pursued in the public schools included not only elementary schools but high schools as well, and a parent was not at liberty to exercise a choice in that regard, and, after his child had graduated from one elementary school and was under sixteen, he could not send it to another elementary school, but must send it to the high school in the township.

Summary

1. The courts have sustained legislation requiring attendance beyond the eighth grade, or the completion of the elementary course, or attendance during years that are usually beyond the time of completing the elementary course. In the four decisions reviewed, parents endeavored in three cases to escape sending their children to school after they had finished the eighth grade, and in one case during the sixteenth year of age. The courts upheld the extension of the school period of compulsory attendance in each case.

2. If fourteen years is accepted as the usual age for completing the eighth grade, it is found that on January 1, 1923, forty states had a higher upper age limit than that. At that time, the legal upper age limit for eight states was fourteen years; for three states fifteen years; for thirty-one states sixteen years; for one state seventeen years; and for five states eighteen years.[42] The significance for education of court decisions upholding such legislation is apparent.

AUTHORITY OF ATTENDANCE OFFICERS

It is obvious that the effectiveness of the enforcement of compulsory attendance at school depends greatly upon the fidelity with which attendance officers perform their duties. It is obvious, too, that if officers felt that in cases of controversy with persons charged with violating the law they would not be sustained by the courts, they would become hesitant and possibly dilatory.

The New York Case.—An action was brought against an attendance officer for malicious prosecution in a county court of New York.[43] The judgment of this court was against the officer,

[42] Bermejo, F. V. *The School Attendance Service in American Cities*, p. 22.
[43] Shappel v. Curtis, 127 N. Y. S. 33. Decided 1911.

and it denied an order for a new trial. From the judgment and the order, the officer appealed to the supreme court.

The attendance officer in the case served also as deputy sheriff of the county. In his attendance district was a child ten years of age, who resided with her mother and regularly attended school until November 11, 1909, when she was expelled therefrom by the principal, pursuant to an order of the board of health, because the mother refused to permit her to be vaccinated. The mother insisted on the admission of the child to school, and continued to send her to the schoolhouse and the school officers persisted in their refusal to admit or receive her until vaccinated. On the 23rd of November, 1909, the attendance officer laid written information before a police justice, in which he stated, among other things, that the mother had not caused the child to attend upon instruction, as required by law; that the child had been absent from instruction nine days between November 11 and November 23, 1909, without legal excuse therefor; and that she had not presented to the school authorities proof by affidavit that she was unable to compel the child to so attend. Acting upon this information, a warrant was issued by the justice to the attendance officer, who arrested the mother, and she was thereafter discharged.

The mother then brought action against the officer in the county court for malicious prosecution. The court charged the jury that the information and warrant had no application to a case of a refusal to provide equivalent instruction elsewhere. He said:

> Mr. Curtis, [the officer] knowing that this woman could not get her children into school because the board of education had excluded them, goes before the justice of the peace and gets out a warrant because she does not send them to school. It seems a peculiar situation to me that a man, knowing that a woman was striving every way she knew how to get her children in the public school, should go and swear out a warrant, charging her with not sending them to public school; but that is just what occurred. The principal fact we have here is that Mr. Curtis did procure this woman to be arrested for an offense which he knew she had not committed.

These extracts, said the supreme court, from the charge of the trial justice show that the case was sent to the jury upon the theory that the charge against the mother, and for which she was arrested, was a failure to cause the child to attend upon instruction at a school, and that the arrest of the mother by the officer was without probable cause. But the information or deposition upon which the warrant was issued, so far as the averment of the commission of an act was concerned, was substantially in the words of the statute. It stated that the mother had not caused the child to attend upon instruction, and that the child had been absent nine days from instruction without excuse. That was the designation of the crime which it was alleged the mother had committed, and the only crime the justice had power to try under the information. There was no pretense that the uncontroverted testimony in this case did not clearly establish a violation of the compulsory education law in that she did not cause the child to attend upon instruction or present proof by affidavit that she was unable to compel her to so attend. It therefore could be said as a matter of law that the officer had probable cause to believe the mother guilty of the crime charged, and that he was fully justified in instituting the proceeding. In other words, the evidence showed, not the want of a probable cause, but the existence of a real cause.

The supreme court held that the judgment and order of the county court should be reversed and a new trial ordered.

Another New York Case.—In another New York case action was brought to recover damages for assault and battery.[44] It was brought by the mother of a boy who was twelve years old at the time of his arrest. The defendant was a school attendance officer of the district. His authority for arresting the boy and taking him to school was found in the education law of the state, which provided that an attendance officer might arrest without warrant a child between seven and sixteen years of age, who was a truant from instruction upon which he was lawfully required to attend within the district of such attendance officer, and forthwith deliver the child to the teacher from whose school he was a truant. The officer went to the house of the mother, where the boy was at the noon hour of December 5, 1916, and attempted to take him to school. The mother interfered, and in the struggle she claimed to have been more or less injured, for which she had brought the action. The case was tried before a county judge and a jury. The jury rendered a verdict in

[44] DeLease v. Nolan, 172 N. Y. S. 552. Decided 1918.

favor of the mother for two hundred fifty dollars. From this verdict, the officer appealed to the supreme court.

In reviewing the case, the supreme court said that it was practically conceded that the mother at first declined to allow the boy to go to school. That the officer put the chain on her arm and twisted it in order to compel her to let go of the boy was not disputed. He may have been fully justified in so doing. She had two doctors called in the day following her injury. They gave her some remedy to rub on the arm which she did not use. She said the Almighty was her physician. Up to the time the chain was put on her arm, the mother had hold of the boy and was trying to prevent the officer's taking him. It did not appear that he applied the chain after she released her hold upon the boy. The officer finally took the boy to school. In the charge, the county court instructed the jury that from the moment the attendance officer placed his hand on the boy in an effort to take him away without his mother's consent, he was a trespasser, and continued so during the further controversy at the mother's premises. The jury might have found from the evidence that the mother resisted the officer in making the arrest, and that he used no more force than was justifiable.

The fact that no physician had attended him, and that he was riding a horse at the time the officer first saw him, having been at a distance of three miles from home on business for his mother on the 5th of December, and also on the day before, was confirmatory of the theory that he was not necessarily out of school by reason of an attack of tonsillitis. During the ten weeks preceding the assault, he attended school only fourteen days, but for the remaining period of nearly eight weeks following the arrest he was in regular attendance.

The defendant was an officer of experience, and was at the time game protector. For six years he had been on the board of water supply police and had risen to the rank of sergeant. He had been attendance officer for about one month. He had received from a lawyer advice as to his duties as an attendance officer. When he reached the schoolhouse that morning, the teacher told him who the delinquents were, and the boy in this case was one of them. The county court charged the jury as follows: "The boy, however, was out of school with the consent of his mother, and the truant officer, as I read the statute, was a trespasser in undertaking to take the child away by force."

The charge proceeded upon the theory that the boy was not a truant. If the parent failed to cause the child to attend, the child was a truant from instruction upon which he was lawfully required to attend. The statute provided that every person standing in the parental relation to a child within the compulsory school age of between seven and fourteen years and between fourteen and sixteen, to whom an employment certificate had not been issued, and who was in proper mental and physical condition, should cause such child to attend school. The state was sovereign in the matter of the attendance of a child at school. The dominion of the state was absolute so far as attendance upon instruction was concerned during the years prescribed in the education law. The consent of the parent to the absence of the child had no effect upon this lawful dominion of the state. Furthermore, the law made it a misdemeanor to interfere with a truant officer in the lawful discharge of his duties. To charge the jury that the officer was a trespasser was an erroneous exposition of the law, and was, of course, fatal to the defense.

The judgment and order of the county court should be reversed, and a new trial granted.

Summary

1. These decisions of the supreme court strengthened the position of attendance officers. They gave the officers assurance of support by the courts, when they were interfered with in the lawful discharge of their duties. The supreme court did not approve the arguments, the points of view, or the construction of the law, which the lower courts adopted, and in both cases reversed their judgments. It is clear that if the decisions of the lower courts had prevailed, the enforcement of the attendance law in New York would have been considerably modified.

2. It is significant that no cases involving the authority of attendance officers are reported from other states. It is significant, too, that no other state specifically provides in its compulsory attendance law that interference with an attendance officer shall be a misdemeanor. It may be assumed that the position of these officers in the discharge of their duties is likely to be less secure in other states than in New York.

WHEN THE COMPULSORY PERIOD BEGINS

A parent was found guilty in a county court of Vermont for violation of the statute against truancy.[45] He appealed to the supreme court.

The chief consideration in this case was the time in the school year that a parent was required by the law to send his child to school. The court stated that the compulsory section of the law was in the nature of a police regulation, and was enacted with a view to the safety and welfare of the state, the intelligence of the people being its safeguard. The school law prescribed that the school year should commence on the first day of April. The court construed the phrase in the law, "beginning with the school year," to mean that the twenty-six weeks of required attendance should commence at the beginning of the first term and be continuous thereafter when the school was in session.

The reasons for the requirement were obvious—that children should begin their attendance when classes were being formed for the year, and that they should not interrupt the work of classes by unnecessary absences. The constitution declared that a competent number of schools ought to be maintained in each town for the convenient instruction of youth, and the statute required that each district should maintain a school at least twenty-eight weeks in the school year, and that all pupils should be thoroughly instructed in certain branches of education. These requirements might be partially defeated and much of the expense of maintaining schools rendered useless, unless regular attendance could be enforced.

The offer of the parent to show that he intended subsequently to send his son to an academy for a period of time which, with the time that he had attended the district school, would make twenty-six continuous weeks was properly excluded by the county court. The offense was committed and he became amenable to the statute whenever it was established that the child was not in attendance upon school in such a manner as would make twenty-six continuous weeks from the beginning of the first term in the school year.

The judgment of the county court was affirmed.

[45] State v. McCaffrey, 69 Vt., 85. Decided 1896.

Summary

1. The court sets forth clearly two reasons for requiring continuous attendance beginning with the first day of school: (*a*) A child should begin work when classes are being formed so as not to interfere with the work of other children by unnecessary absences. The individual may not act in such a way as to endanger the welfare of the group to which he belongs. (*b*) Districts are required by law to maintain schools a definite period of time. These provisions by the state for educating children might be defeated, and the money spent for maintaining schools be lost, if regular attendance were not enforced.

2. For these reasons the court construes strictly the beginning time as the first day of school. It does not permit a parent the discretion of making up time lost at the beginning of the public school year by sending his child to a private school after public school is out.

EXCUSES FOR NONATTENDANCE

An issue that was decided in a Pennsylvania case concerned the question of who were the proper judges of excuses for nonattendance.[46] A parent had been convicted before an alderman for violating the compulsory education law. He appealed to the district court for a new trial and an arrest of judgment. These were denied.

The parent took exception to the refusal of the alderman's court to permit him to present to the jury, as a defense in the case, certain alleged excuses for keeping his child out of school, which the school law required him to produce before the board of school directors, and of the truth and sufficiency of which it made the board the judge,—it having been proven, and was an undisputed fact, that the parent had been repeatedly notified to appear before the board at specified times for that purpose, and that he had utterly ignored such notification.

The district court argued that obviously the objects of the compulsory education law could not be accomplished in any way except by requiring excuses for nonattendance to be submitted to and determined by the board. What would constitute a sufficient excuse in one locality, for example, in a sparsely

[46] Commonwealth v. Hammer, 9 Pa. D. R. 251. Decided 1899.

settled rural district, where distances were great and roads in some seasons difficult, might not be a good excuse in another locality where the conditions were altogether different. The local board was manifestly the proper body to pass upon such questions. If, in every case, a jury taken from dissimilar localities could either be substituted in the place of the board to pronounce in the first instance upon the sufficiency of alleged excuses, or, the board having passed upon them, be appealed to for a reversal of its decision, the law itself would be paralyzed and its execution practically frustrated.

Summary

1. This case indicates that requiring excuses from parents for absences is important in the enforcement of attendance. If such excuses may not be required by the local authorities and their sufficiency judged by them, the requirements of the law as to attendance may be evaded. The decision of the court set aside any possibility of such evasion.

2. Few of the states recognize the importance of provisions for requiring and judging excuses to the extent of making specific mention of them in the attendance laws. Texas provides that excuses must be in writing and signed by the parents of the children.[47] South Carolina has the most explicit provisions of the states that mention excuses at all. Each teacher shall report monthly all absences, together with excuses for such absences, showing which have previously been reported, and which have been excused by the teacher. No teacher's pay shall be approved by trustees unless such report is attached. The trustees shall consider the absences excused by the teacher; if, in their opinion, the excuse is not sufficient, they shall report so to the superintendent of education, who shall proceed as in cases of unexcused absences.[48] Six other states mention absences, but leave the matter of requiring excuses from parents to be implied. In Nebraska, the teachers shall report causes of absence.[49] In Pennsylvania, teachers shall report children absent three days without lawful excuse.[50] In Alabama, teachers shall report weekly the names of children of compul-

[47] Texas School Laws, 1925.
[48] South Carolina School Laws, 1924.
[49] Nebraska School Laws, 1925.
[50] Pennsylvania School Laws, 1923.

sory age absent without satisfactory excuse.[51] In Delaware, children are excused by the superintendent according to rules and regulations of the state board of education for necessary and legal absences.[52] In Louisiana, truancy is defined as absence from school without reasonable excuse.[53] In Maine, a habitual truant is defined as a child absent without sufficient excuse five day sessions or ten half-day sessions in any period of six months.[54]

3. No state in its school laws on attendance has made specific provisions for requiring parents to send excuses for tardiness. Yet promptness, as well as regularity, is recognized in the court decisions as a necessary element in the satisfactory compliance with attendance requirements. It may be that excuses for both absence and tardiness are in some cases properly provided for by local authorities under the general legislative grant of power to make the necessary rules and regulations for the government of the schools. It is likely, however, that in many, if not most districts, the local board does not make use of this grant of power in such specific way that teachers may rely upon the unvarying exercise of it. Specific state legislation requiring parents to give written excuses for both tardiness and absence, and providing that the local school authorities shall judge the sufficiency of the excuses, and providing further that the county superintendent shall check such excuses for rural schools, would operate to secure a better degree of enforcement of the attendance laws.

PUNISHMENT FOR CONTEMPT

A case came to the supreme court of Washington on appeal from a superior court.[55] On complaint of a county superintendent, a man and wife had been cited before the superior court of the county to show cause why they did not send their three minor children to the common school in the district in which the parents resided. The parents were commanded to bring the three children into court for examination as to their proficiency in the course of education prescribed in the common

[51] Alabama School Laws, 1924.
[52] Delaware School Laws, 1923.
[53] Louisiana School Laws, 1923.
[54] Maine School Laws, 1925.
[55] State Ex. Rel. Henry v. McDonald, 25 Wash. 122. Decided 1901.

schools. At the hearing, the children were examined and the reason of the parents for not sending them to school ascertained. The court peremptorily ordered the parents to send the children to the school in session in the district. This order they did not comply with. They were then held as for contempt, and punished by a fine of twenty dollars each, and in default of payment of such fine they should stand committed to the custody of the sheriff of the county until the fine was paid or they be discharged in pursuance of law. Judgment also for the costs of the entire proceedings was rendered against them.

The question before the supreme court, on the appeal from the above judgment, was the power of the superior court to inflict the judgment for contempt. The supreme court decided that the only penalty permitted by the law in cases of violation of the compulsory education law, which violation consisted of failure of a parent to give a satisfactory cause for not keeping his children in school, was a fine in the sum of not less than ten dollars nor more than twenty-five dollars for each offense. No power was specifically given to the judge of the superior court to punish as contempt a refusal to comply with the order of the court to send children to school. It might be safely assumed that no such power to punish by contempt existed at common law, and the statute did not attempt to give such authority. The judgment of the lower court was, therefore, reversed and direction given to dismiss the proceeding.

Summary

1. The specific functions of courts in enforcing compulsory attendance laws, as stated in the enactments, are to hear and determine cases involving violation of the attendance laws and impose the punishments provided by law. Determining the degree of guilt and imposing punishments that will secure conformity with the law are major functions of courts in attendance cases. The above decision definitely fixes the limits of punishment permitted to a court.

RELATION OF CHILD LABOR TO COMPULSORY EDUCATION

The relation of child labor and of child labor legislation to enforced attendance is clearly set forth in a New York case.[56]

[56] City of New York v. Chelsea Jute Mills, 88 N. Y. S. 1085. Decided 1904.

A child was employed in a manufacturing establishment in the city of New York. She was twelve years old on July 29, 1903, began work in the factory on April 7, 1903, and continued until the day preceding the trial. She worked from 7 A.M. to 6:15 P.M., with forty-five minutes off at noon, except that on Saturday she ceased work at 2:15 P.M. When she applied for work on April 7, 1903, she stated that she was past sixteen, and gave the forelady an affidavit signed and sworn to by her father on April 6, 1903, before a commissioner of deeds to the effect that she was born on April 4, 1887, and that she was sixteen years old April 4, 1903. On trial, the father testified that the affidavit was not true, but that July 29, 1903, was her twelfth birthday. The mother testified the same. There was no objection to this testimony as to age.

This case was tried in a municipal court of the city of New York in March, 1904. It was the first case of its kind in the state. It was regarded as a test case, upon the outcome of which many others depended. It had a definite relation to compulsory attendance; hence, its great importance.

The language of the statute under which the case was brought was:

> It shall be unlawful for any person, firm, or corporation to employ any child under fourteen years of age in any business or service whatever, during any part of the term during which the public schools of the district in which the child resides are in session; . . . and any person who shall employ any child contrary to the provision of this section . . . shall for each offense forfeit and pay to the treasurer of the city or village or to the supervisor of the town in which such child resides a penalty of fifty dollars.

Under this law, the company that employed the child in the case became the defendant before the court. The defendant assailed the statute as unconstitutional. It claimed the law was an unwarranted, illegal, and unconstitutional deprivation of its liberties. It urged immunity from the penalty on account of the alleged good faith of the company, absence of intent to violate the statute, and nonemployment of the child since her age was established in the court. The court upheld the integrity of the statute under the police power of the state. Every presumption was in favor of the constitutionality of the statute. The police power included such legislative measures as promote the health, safety, or morals of the community. It was true that the legislature must respect freedom of contract, and the right to live and work where and how one would. Yet the weal of the people was the supreme law. The legislature might not disregard it; private interests were subordinate to the public good, and even a statute opposed to natural justice and equity, requiring vigilance or causing vexation or annoyance would be upheld if within constitutional limitations. Much more potent, if possible, was a statute seeking the protection of children. They were the wards of the state, which was particularly interested in their well-being as future members of the body politic and had an inherent right to protect itself and them against the baneful effects of ignorance, infirmity, or danger to life and limb.

The courts had declared that the legislature had the right and power to exercise its judgment as to what would be detrimental to the best interests of the children of the state, and, having done so, such judgment should not be impeached by the court, and that it could not be disputed that the interest which the state had in the physical, moral, and intellectual well-being of its members warranted the implication and the exercise of every just power which would result in preparing the child in future life to support itself, to serve the state, and in all relations and duties of adult life to perform well and capably its part. So statutes had been passed providing for compulsory vaccination of children, and had been upheld as within the police power.

The statute under consideration did not discriminate; it was auxiliary to the primary purpose to enforce education and elevate future citizenship; it was not arbitrary, put no unnecessary restriction on the freedom of action, and resorted to no unnecessary rigor, because it would be impossible, otherwise than by an absolute prohibition of employment of all children under fourteen years of age, to accomplish its beneficent ends. It did not constitute any improper infringement of any right a parent might have in the child or its labor, or a child might have to labor. In its effort to test the validity of an act, the court was not confined to the statute itself, its general scope and trends, or literal provisions. The court might resort to facts and circumstances of which it might take judicial notice, and evidence might be introduced to enlighten the judicial mind. There was no dearth of medical testimony as to the evils of child labor.

The annual reports of the factory inspectors called attention in strong terms to the evils of child labor, and the necessity of compulsory education.

The objection that the child labor law was foreign to the scope of the school law, and in no way aided the school authorities in their work and had no legitimate place in that statute, was not tenable. The provisions of the child labor law must be read in connection with the compulsory school law, which was complementary to and a necessary concomitant of the former. They emphasized the intent of the legislature to prohibit the labor and enforce the education of children under the stated age; in no other way could its salutary purpose have been more effectually encompassed. The labor law was directly germane to the chief end of the school law. The legislature reaffirmed its mandate against child labor to foster education, upon the benign theory that representative government could be safe only when future suffrage was enlightened by education.

The defendant might not assert exemption from liability on account of good faith, want of intent to violate the statute, and nonemployment of the child since the trial. Assuredly, the last ground was not seriously urged. If it were countenanced, the extent and duration of violations of the statute would only be measured by a defendant's successful appeal to the law's delay. The good faith of the defendant and absence of intent was not an excuse. The defendant was not active in its quest after the age of the child. It was passive. It complacently received the affidavit of the father upon the point. The forelady testified that she made no inquiries, but rested entirely upon the affidavit and the statement of the girl that she was sixteen past.

The present statute was absolute. It must necessarily be so to accomplish its object. The employer acted at his peril. The fact of employment made him liable. The contention of the defendant would require judicial legislation and render the statute nugatory, for good faith could easily be alleged and seldom disproved. The rule was well established that unless a statute made knowledge and intent elements of its violation, neither the want of knowledge nor the absence of intent could be shown as a defense.

The legislature must be presumed to have deliberately passed an act which would not nullify itself. If this law were declared invalid, the door would be thrown wide open to the most noxious kinds of child labor.

Judgment was given against the defendant, who was fined fifty dollars with costs and disbursements.

Summary

1. The following principles for the guidance of parents, employers, and school authorities were established in this decision:

A. The state had an inherent right to protect itself and the children in the state, who were its wards, from the effects of ignorance, infirmity, or danger to life and limb.

B. Legislation to prevent child labor was auxiliary to the primary purpose to enforce education; one was complementary to the other.

C. Prevention of child labor was no improper infringement of any right of a parent, child, or employer.

D. Good faith or want of intent to violate the statute was no defense for the employer.

.2. This decision was rendered more than twenty years ago. It is remarkable that it is the only decision of its kind to be found in the references. Since 1904, no employer in any state where a child labor law is operative has permitted an issue to arise to the point of opposing the law in the courts, or if it has been tried in lower courts, has not carried it to higher courts of record. In the legislation on which the decision is based "the interests of the child and of society have first place. Needy parents may no longer jeopardize the future of the state by denying to their children the elements of an education. Employers have discovered that, after all, the labor of young children is not so profitable as had been supposed, and in case of illegal employment there is little opportunity for refuge in the ambiguous or confusing phrasing of statutes." [57]

3. The responsibility of the employer was affirmed in a very positive way in this decision. The language of the court was that "the employer acted at his peril. The fact of employment made him liable." To establish such a principle in legislation and have it strongly upheld in the courts represents vast progress since the labor-attendance legislation in Massachusetts in 1842. Then the prosecution must prove that the employer had

[57] Ensign, F. C. *Compulsory School Attendance and Child Labor*, p. 234.

"knowingly" employed a child under the restricted age. The use of this word in child labor legislation for a half century after had the effect of protecting the employer and making evasion of the purpose of the law possible.[58]

4. The facts in this case disclose the necessity for legislation covering:

A. Proof of age.
B. Punishment for falsifying concerning age or employment.
C. Record of schooling.
D. Certificate of employment.

TRANSPORTATION AND COMPULSORY ATTENDANCE

In a New Hampshire case, the responsibility of a parent who lived at a distance from school to convey his child to school was involved.[59] The parent and child resided three miles from a schoolhouse in the district where a public school was annually taught. It was unreasonable to require the child to walk that distance, and no transportation was provided by the school board. The board set aside twenty-five per cent of the school money for the conveyance of scholars, and offered the parent a proportionate part of that sum to convey his child to and from school. The parent declined to accept the sum offered and refused to transport the child. The board was unable to procure transportation for the sum offered the parent. The rate offered him for the service was the same paid for the conveyance of other scholars in the district where such conveyance was required. Under these circumstances the father was indicted for not causing his child eleven years old to attend school as required by law. He was found guilty in a superior court and appealed to the state supreme court.

The court here argued that the legislature did not intend to imprison or fine a parent who had not the means to secure conveyance for his child. The purpose of the law was the education of the child. Accordingly, the existing statute provided:

> The school board of every district shall provide schools at such places within the district . . . as will best subserve the interests of education and will give to all the scholars of the district as nearly equal advantages as may be practicable. They may use a portion of the school money, not

[58] *Ibid.*, p. 49.
[59] State v. Hall, 74 N. H. 61. Decided 1906.

exceeding twenty-five per cent, for the purpose of conveying scholars to and from the schools.

If the school board were able to so arrange the schools as to give all the scholars reasonably equal advantages, they might by providing conveyance render such advantages as nearly equal as practicable. But if, as the schools had been arranged, the amount of expenditure permitted for that purpose was insufficient to provide the necessary transportation, the remedy was to be found in an additional number of schools, which would require less expenditure for the conveyance of scholars.

The case contained facts conflicting as evidence upon the question whether the school board offered the parent reasonable payment for the conveyance of his child. Whether the sum offered was or was not reasonably sufficient was immaterial. The parent was under no more legal obligation to convey his child for reasonable compensation than he was to convey another child in the district, nor was a greater duty to engage in this business placed on him because of his child than upon any other inhabitant who had no child. The statute did not require the parent to furnish to the district conveyance of scholars at his own expense, or for the sum thought reasonable by the school board. The facts, agreed upon, that the child could not reasonably be required to walk and that no conveyance had been provided by the school board, constituted a defense to the indictment.

Summary

1. A principle established in this decision is that there are definite limits to the amount of responsibility that a parent can be compelled to assume in meeting the requirements of the attendance law. If the parent lived beyond the distance fixed by law from school, the responsibility of providing a way for the education of his children rested not on him but on the state. It was the responsibility of the state, when the question of distance was involved, either to furnish conveyance or more schools. If the state failed to do these things, the parent could not be punished for a violation of the compulsory attendance law.

2. A definite limit as to distance is set in the attendance laws of eighteen states. In addition, in some of these states different limits are set for different ages. There are five limits specified:

one and a half miles, two miles, two and one-fourth miles, two and a half miles, and three miles. One and a half miles is the limit in Oregon for children nine and ten years old. Two miles is the limit in California, Pennsylvania, Virginia, West Virginia, Wisconsin for children under nine, in Florida for children seven to nine, and in South Carolina for children under twelve. Two and one-fourth miles is the limit in North Dakota; families beyond this distance are paid from twenty-five cents to fifty cents a day for transportation, depending on distance and number of children in family attending school. Two and a half miles is the limit in Alabama, Louisiana, Mississippi, Texas, Utah, Michigan for children under nine, and in South Carolina for children over twelve. Three miles is the limit in Nebraska, New Mexico, Tennessee, Florida for children ten to eighteen, in Oregon for children over ten, and in Wisconsin for children nine to fourteen, who shall attend at least sixty days during the year.

3. Minnesota specifies no definite limit but exempts children who have "no school within reasonable distance." Likewise, Nevada exempts children who live "at such distance as to render attendance impracticable or unsafe." And Montana provides that "the county superintendent may excuse where distance makes an undue hardship."

4. In thirteen of the eighteen states in which definite limits are set, the provision is made that exemption applies only in case free transportation is not furnished.

WHAT CONSTITUTES ATTENDANCE AT SCHOOL

A parent was arrested on a charge of failing, neglecting, and refusing to cause his child of compulsory school age to attend school.[60] The parent's religious faith caused him to be opposed to defending his country in time of war. He instructed his child not to take the pledge of allegiance and give the flag salute, and if she was sent from the room by the teacher for refusing to obey the rule as to the exercises, to stay out until after the noon recess and then go to school again. This happened daily until the parent's arrest.

The law of the state provided that whenever any child of school age was out of school, the truant officer should notify the parent to cause the child to attend some recognized school within

[60] Trayer v. State, 21 Ohio N. P. (N.S.) 121. Decided 1918.

two days from the date of the notice, and it should be the duty of the parent so to cause its attendance at some recognized school.

The parent was tried twice on the above charge in the court of the mayor of the village. At the first trial he pleaded guilty and was fined with costs, which he paid. At the second trial, he was charged with a second offense, was convicted and sentenced to twenty-five days in jail. He appealed to the common pleas court of the county.

This court held that the statute was not complied with when a parent sent a child to the schoolhouse or the schoolroom. The law was that such person "cause the child to attend school." The reason for the truant law, and the requirement that adults having the care and custody of children cause them to attend school was that the children might escape illiteracy and that they might receive education.

The case was one where the child was trying to serve two masters. The child said that the father told her not to salute the flag. She was put in fear by the command at home, and, as between the two masters, chose to be sent, harmless in the corporal sense, from the schoolroom. Under such circumstances, the child could not be condemned as incorrigible. In order to manifest the father's spirit of rebellion, the child was deprived of her right to attend school and receive proper instruction and education.

The sentence of the court below was upheld.

Summary

1. In this decision, attendance at school was defined as including participation in the usual work and exercises of the school. The law which provided that a parent "shall cause his child to attend school" placed a responsibility on the parent for the attitude and conduct of the child during the school sessions. If the child was not responsive to the instruction of the teacher, the parent could be punished for violating the attendance law, provided the lack of responsiveness was his fault.

DEFENSE FOR NONATTENDANCE

What constituted a defense for nonattendance was the issue involved in a case first tried before a justice of the peace and a jury in the state of New York.[61] On trial, a parent was convicted of violating the education law and was fined five dollars. He appealed to the county court. This parent, who had two children physically and mentally able to attend school, lived three and one-half miles from school by one road, and one mile two-hundred-ninety rods by a shorter road which had water standing in it in places during rainy weather. Prior to February, 1919, transportation had been furnished by the school district for these children to and from school, but in that month the transportation was discontinued by the district. Thereafter, the parent failed to cause his children to attend school. Distance and bad roads for part of the time were the parent's excuse for not sending his children to school at all.

The county court held that the only defense in a prosecution under the law providing for compulsory education of children between eight and sixteen was that they were not in proper physical and mental condition to attend school. The education law was not unreasonable. It provided that parents might cause their children to attend upon instruction other than in public schools. It provided also that "occasional absences from school attendance, not amounting to irregular attendance in the fair meaning of the term, should be allowed upon such excuses only as would be allowed in like cases by the general rules and practice of such public school." But when a parent refused to perform his duty of causing his child to attend upon such instruction of any sort, then he violated the law in both letter and spirit and incurred the penalty provided by the law.

The excuse of the parent that the distance from his house to the schoolhouse was too great, and that the roads for part of the time were so bad that it would be unreasonable to require him to send his children, should be presented by proper petition to the state board of education, or by an appeal from the decision of the school district to discontinue the transportation of school children.

The judgment of the lower court was affirmed.

Summary

1. Under this decision, the attendance of children within the compulsory age limits upon instruction is mandatory. To escape

[61] People v. Himmonen, 178 N. Y. S. 282. Decided 1919.

responsibility for such instruction, the parent must prove physical or mental incapacity for attendance. Such a condition constitutes the only legal exemption. The decision acknowledges that the state has a responsibility when the matter of distance from school is involved and that the parent may petition state authorities for relief.

2. The elimination of easy exemptions from attendance on instruction represents a phase of the growing sentiment to secure adequate education for all children of the state. However, a good many easy exemptions are still specified in the attendance laws. Seven states provide exemptions in case the child must support the parent; three in case of poverty of parent; one where attendance is a hardship; one in case of extreme emergency; one for reasons sufficient to the court; one for cause acceptable to the attendance officer.

RESPONSIBILITY OF PARENTS

A juvenile court in Wisconsin found that a boy twelve years of age, who had been frequently absent from school, was habitually truant; that he was incorrigible and delinquent; and that a due regard for the morals and welfare of the boy required that he be committed to the state industrial school for boys.[62] From this order, the father appealed to the supreme court.

In the opinion of the court, the law contemplated that the parent should first be proceeded against, if for any reason a child within his care and custody did not comply with the law relating to compulsory school attendance. There was no evidence in this case that the truant officer, the school authorities, or any one else had called the attention of the father of the boy to the fact that he was not attending school, and the evidence did show that when he was absent he was at work, at least a part of the time. The statute did not define the words "habitually truant." The evidence came far short in this case of establishing the sort of habitual truancy upon which a finding of delinquency might be based. The habitual truancy which amounted to delinquency was a refusal to attend school in defiance of parental authority. It was the purpose and intention of the statute that the child should not be held a truant, except in cases where the parent was unable to compel compliance by his child with

[62] In re: Alley, 182 N. W., 360. Decided 1921.

the provisions of the compulsory school attendance law. The child in this case, if he could properly be said to be a truant at all—which was very doubtful in view of the fact that his absence was consented to by his father—was far from being habitually truant within the meaning of the law.

It might well be that there were parents in the state who did not fully understand the purpose and objects of the recent legislation in regard to the education, protection, and reformation of children, and that such legislation imposed upon parents a positive duty and a much higher obligation than that under which many parents supposed themselves to labor. The parent no longer had the right to decide whether his child should attend school or work; the law determined that for him.

The order of the juvenile court was reversed with directions.

Summary

1. In committing this boy of twelve to the state industrial school, the lower court was proceeding on the assumption that the boy was responsible for his acts and that the parent was not. This was done, too, without proof of whether the parent was responsible or not. The supreme court made clear the principle that parental responsibility must be assumed until the parent proves inability to control the child, in which case the parent may be discharged from responsibility and from penalty for the child's conduct. An important principle in enforcing compulsory attendance is not only assuming parental responsibility but inducing parents to assume it more fully and to execute it more effectively.

MAY DEFENDANTS SELECT THE MAGISTRATE?

In 1923, the legislature of Tennessee undertook to amend the compulsory school laws in their application to counties having a population of not less than 23,250, and not more than 23,300.[63] This restricted the proposed amendment to only one county of the state—Claiborne County. The Act contained the following provision:

> And in case of any prosecution the defendant at all times shall select the magistrate of the civil district in which he lives to try his case, and the officer notifying or summoning such parent, guardian, or custodian of any

[63] Ford v. State, 263 S. W. 60. Decided 1924.

school child or children for prosecution, shall inquire of such defendant what magistrate of his district he wishes to be tried before, and the summoning shall be returned accordingly.

Under this law a case came before the Claiborne County circuit court which declared the law unconstitutional. The defendant appealed to the supreme court, which quoted the general school law of the state as providing that: "Any justice of the peace or juvenile judge shall be vested with the power to hear all cases coming within the provisions of this Act." The court could conceive of no reason why citizens of Claiborne County violating this law should be entitled to pick their magistrate before whom to be tried, when citizens of other counties of the state must be tried before "any justice of the peace or juvenile court judge." Such discrimination could not be justified upon any reasonable grounds. On the contrary, it was palpably vicious, and not to be maintained on a population or any other basis. A corrupt or biased magistrate might destroy the entire benefit of the school law in his district if the act before the court were upheld.

Summary

1. In such a case of special legislation, no other final decision than the one rendered is conceivable. Incidentally, the court expresses a fact which on occasion may be very important in its effect on the enforcement of the law. This fact is that a judge may destroy the benefit of the school law in his district. Since this lies within the discretion of the judge, it must be assumed, on the other hand, that a judge may increase the effectiveness of the school law in his district. In general, the attitude of the courts is an important element in the enforcement of school attendance.

STATE MUST PROVE OFFENSE

A parent was convicted before a justice of the peace in North Carolina of a violation of the compulsory attendance law.[64] The warrant of the justice charged that the parent had failed or refused to send his children of compulsory age to the public school in his district as required by the laws of North Carolina. The parent appealed from the judgment of the justice of the

[64] State v. Johnson, 125 S. E. 183. Decided 1924.

peace to the superior court of the county. Here he demurred to the warrant and moved to quash same in that it failed to charge a criminal offense. The motion was overruled; the plea of not guilty was entered, evidence was submitted, and the defendant was convicted in this court. He appealed to the supreme court.

The supreme court quoted the statute on which the prosecution was based as follows:

> Every person, guardian, or other person in the state having charge or control of a child between the ages of eight and fourteen years shall cause such child to attend school continuously for a period equal to the time which the public school in the district in which the child resides shall be in session. The principal, superintendent, or teacher who is in charge of such school shall have the right to excuse the child from temporary attendance on account of sickness or distance of residence from the school, or other unavoidable cause which does not constitute truancy as defined by the state board of education.

The court pointed out that the statute did not make the failure to cause the attendance of children in the public schools a crime, but defined the offense as a failure on the part of the parent or guardian or persons having control of the children of the specified ages to cause them to attend "school" continuously for a period equal to the time the public schools of the district should be in session. In the warrant, the defendant was charged only with a failure to cause attendance in the public schools; it did not, therefore, contain the charge of a criminal offense, and should have been quashed or amended so as to state properly and sufficiently the charge insisted upon by the state.

The defect in the warrant of the justice might have been cured by amendment on motion made in the superior court. But the difficulty in this case was that the same objection appeared in the charges of the court on the trial of the issues before the jury. Thus the court instructed the jury among other things:

> Now, if you find the facts to be as shown by the evidence, Gentlemen, you will find that under the law as to public schools, the defendant was required to send his children to school, the public school in his district.
>
> If the defendant relies upon his having sent his children to some other school than the school in question, the burden is upon him to show that, or, if he relies upon his children's being out of school on account of any legal excuse, the burden is upon him to show that. That is a matter peculiarly within his knowledge, and the burden is not upon the state to show that the defendant sent his children to any other school and that is a matter of defense for the defendant to show. If the state has shown that

there was a public school being conducted in his district, an eight-month term, and that he has failed to send his children to this school and has violated this statute, nothing else appearing, then the defendant would be guilty.

The supreme court had heretofore shown that in criminal prosecutions it was required that the charge should state the essentials of the offense, and what it was necessary to allege as a general rule must be proved, and that beyond a reasonable doubt. It was recognized that in certain instances, when a statute created a distinct and substantive criminal offense, the description of the same being complete and definite, and by proviso in the same or subsequent clause a certain case or class of cases was withdrawn from the effect and operation of the statute, a defendant who sought protection by reason of the exemption and as to matters relating to him personally or peculiarly within his personal knowledge had the burden of showing that he came within the same. But in the case before the court, no such conditions were presented. There was no proviso or exception in this law. On the contrary, the statute made it an offense when there was a failure on the part of parents or guardians to cause children of specified ages under their control to attend school for a period equal to the time the public schools were taught in the district where the children resided, and in such cases all the authorities were to the effect that the substantial features of the offense must be set forth in the warrant or bill of indictment, and must be proved as alleged beyond a reasonable doubt.

There was error in the charge specified; for a defendant was not put on explanation by mere proof of failure of children under his control to attend a public school; and until there were facts in evidence permitting the inference of a failure to attend any properly conducted and recognized school for the time required and during a scholastic year, there could be no valid conviction of the offense.

The judgment of the lower court was reversed and a new trial ordered.

Summary

1. Attendance at public school is not requisite as a compliance with the law. Other instruction will fulfill the demands of the law.

2. The burden of proof was not on the parent to show that he was providing other instruction than the public school for his children.

3. The burden was on the state to charge and to prove that the parent was not providing his children with lawful instruction.

4. This case was tried in three courts before the controversy was regarded as settled. It doubtless represents the expenditure of a great deal of time, effort, and money on the part of a number of people. Yet it was all due to the defect of one word in the warrant drawn up by the justice of the peace. This entire litigation might have been obviated by a law requiring the state department of education to prepare and distribute such legal forms.

GENERAL SUMMARY

1. Judicial decisions in courts of record in cases affecting compulsory attendance are relatively few in number. The sources gave only forty-six cases of this kind.

2. Most of the decisions have been rendered in recent years, more than eighty per cent having been rendered since 1900.

3. Fewer than half of the states have records of decisions in attendance cases. Nearly one-third of all the decisions were confined to Pennsylvania and New York.

4. A classification of the cases in these decisions under the general question that each dealt with shows seventeen such questions or subjects.

5. The constitutionality of compulsory education enactments has been upheld in every case in which that question was the issue. For nearly twenty-five years, this question has not been raised in a court of record in any state. Every state in the union now has a compulsory education law.

6. Courts of record have held that rules and regulations by school boards requiring regular and prompt attendance are reasonable and proper. No decisions on this subject have been required for forty years. State-wide laws on compulsory attendance have obviated the necessity of such rules and regulations by local school authorities.

7. More litigation has been had over the question of compulsory attendance as related to vaccination than over any other

of the seventeen questions of controversy. Eleven decisions have been rendered in such cases, ranging in time from 1900 to 1919. The latest decisions in New York and Pennsylvania support the principle that unvaccinated children must be excluded from public schools and that the parents of such children can escape punishment under the attendance laws only by providing private instruction satisfactory to the school authorities.

8. Private and parochial school instruction are upheld by the courts. The states may supervise such instruction in a reasonable way, but legislation requiring children of the compulsory age to attend only public schools is not constitutional.

9. Decisions of the courts have been necessary to construe the words of the law stating the age limits of attendance. The necessity for such decisions could be obviated by using birthdays for fixing definite limits. Only one state in its legislation uses the birthdays for fixing the age limits.

10. Legislation requiring attendance at school beyond the eighth grade, or beyond the age of fourteen years, has been sustained by the courts.

11. The supreme court of New York has rendered decisions in which the position of attendance officers, who have been interfered with in the discharge of their duties, has been strengthened. No other state reports similar decisions and no other state has specific legislation making interference with an attendance officer a misdemeanor.

12. Legislation requiring continuous attendance beginning with the first day of school has been sustained by the courts on the grounds that children may not interfere by late entrance with the progress of other children, and that since the state requires the maintenance of schools by the district, attendance by the children must be consecutive in order not to defeat the purposes of the state in imposing such a requirement on the district.

13. The courts have held that local authorities may require from parents written excuses for the absence of their children, and may judge the sufficiency of such excuses. Few of the states have specific legislation bearing on the excuses for the absence of children. No state has made specific provisions that require parents to send excuses for tardiness. Wider legislation bearing on excuses both for absence and tardiness would

operate to secure a better degree of observance of the attendance laws.

14. Only one case involving the relation of child labor to compulsory education was found. The decision in this case was rendered more than twenty years ago. It established the principle that the employer acted at his peril in employing children. In other words, he must know that he is employing a person legally qualified to work, otherwise he is subject to penalty.

15. The courts have sustained the principle that there are definite limits of distance beyond which parents cannot be compelled to assume responsibility for meeting the requirements of the attendance law. If parents lived beyond the distance fixed by law, the responsibility of providing a way for the education of their children rested on the state either by furnishing transportation, building additional schools, or exempting the children from attendance.

16. Attendance at school has been defined by the courts as including participation in the usual work and exercises of the school, and parents are held responsible for such participation by their children.

17. The elimination from state laws of easy exemptions from attendance is a necessary condition to secure adequate education for all children of the state. In one state, the court sustained the view that the only legal exemption was proven physical or mental incapacity for attendance.

18. The courts have held that parental responsibility for the child's conduct must be assumed until the parent proves that the child is beyond control.

19. The attitude of the courts is an important element in the enforcement of attendance at school. It is within the discretion of the judge so to apply a law as to destroy the benefit of its enforcement in his district.

20. Some litigation affecting the enforcement of the attendance laws might have been obviated by requiring state departments of education to prepare and distribute the legal forms on which the charges of violation of such laws are made.

CHAPTER IV

PROVISIONS FOR COURT FUNCTIONS IN STATE ATTENDANCE LAWS

SOURCES

For this part of this study, the latest state school laws available in the library of Teachers College, Columbia University, were used. Table 1 gives the years of publication of these laws, and lists for each year the states which published school laws. Most of the laws were published in the years 1923 and 1925.

TABLE 1

STATE SCHOOL LAWS USED AND YEARS OF PUBLICATION

Year of Publication	States	Number
1917	Colo.	1
1920	Ark.	1
1921	Ill., Mass., N. Dak., N. J., N. Y.	5
1922	Conn., Ky., Md., Ohio	4
1923	Calif., Del., Fla., Ga., Ind., Kans., La., Minn., Mont., Mo., Mich., Nev., N. H., N. Y., Pa., R. I., S. Dak., Va., W. Va., Wis., Wash.	21
1924	Ala., Miss., S. C., Tex.	4
1925	Ariz., Ida., Iowa, Me., Nebr., N. Mex., N. C., Okla., Ore., Tenn., Utah, Vt.	12

From these laws, a compilation was made of the items pertaining to compulsory education. The compilation for each state was then sent on January 14, 1926, to the state department of education of that state with the request that it be corrected or any additions by way of recent legislation be appended. The compilations were all returned with the necessary changes made. It may be said, therefore, that the laws used for this study were the laws operative up to the date of January 14, 1926.

COURTS SPECIFIED IN THE STATE LAWS

An analysis of the state compulsory attendance laws shows that twenty-three different designations are used to indicate

TABLE 2

COURTS SPECIFIED IN STATE LAWS AS HAVING JURISDICTION IN CASES INVOLVING COMPULSORY ATTENDANCE

States	Justice of the Peace	Juvenile Court	Court of Competent Jurisdiction	Police Court	County Court	Judge of the City Court	Circuit Court	District Court	Recorder of City	Superior Court of the County	Trial Justice	Magistrate	Recorder of the County	Probate Court	Nearest Court Having Jurisdiction	Mayor	Any Court Having Jurisdiction of Misdemeanors	Proper Court	Courts of Special Sessions	Court of Common Pleas of County	Alderman	Court of Quarter Sessions	Domestic Relations Court	No Court Specified	Total for Each State
Ala.			x																						1
Ariz.			x																						1
Ark.			x																						1
Calif.	x								x				x												3
Colo.					x																				1
Conn.	x			x		x																			3
Del.	x									x															2
Fla.			x																						1
Ga.																								x	1
Idaho														x											1
Ill.	x																								1
Ind.		x					x			x															3
Iowa																								x	1
Kans.		x	x																						2
Ky.															x										1
La.		x	x																						2
Me.				x		x					x														3
Md.	x	x																							2
Mass.		x						x			x														3
Mich.	x																								1
Minn.																	x								1
Miss.	x			x												x									3
Mo.	x				x		x											x							4
Mont.			x																						1
Nebr.		x																							1
Nev.																								x	1
N. H.																								x	1
N. J.		x		x					x																3
N. Mex.	x							x																	2
N. Y.				x															x	x					3
N. C.		x																							1
N. Dak.	x			x																					2
Ohio		x	x																						2
Okla.	x	x			x																				3
Ore.	x																								1
Pa.	x	x										x									x	x			5
R. I.		x						x																	
S. C.												x													
S. Dak.					x		x																		
Tenn.	x	x			x	x	x		x																
Tex.	x	x			x																				
Utah		x						x																	
Vt.																								x	
Va.	x	x		x		x	x																x		6
Wash.	x					x				x															3
W. Va.	x																								1
Wis.	x	x																							2
Wyo.	x							x																	2
Total	20	17	8	7	6	5	5	5	3	3	2	2	1	1	1	1	1	1	1	1	1	1	1	5	—

courts having jurisdiction in attendance cases. Table 2 gives the distribution of the courts by states. Table 3 gives the names of the courts in the order of frequency, or the number of states in which each court is specified as having jurisdiction. Table 4 shows the number of states specifying various numbers of

TABLE 3

NUMBER OF STATES SPECIFYING EACH COURT IN ATTENDANCE CASES

COURT	NUMBER OF STATES
Justice of the Peace	20
Juvenile Court	17
Police Court	7
Court of Competent Jurisdiction	8
County Court	6
Circuit Court	5
District Court	5
Judge of the City Court	5
Recorder of the City	3
Superior Court of County	3
Trial Justice	2
Magistrate	2
Recorder of County	1
Probate Court	1
Nearest Court Having Jurisdiction	1
Mayor	1
Any Court Having Jurisdiction of Misdemeanors	1
Proper Court	1
Courts of Special Sessions	1
Court of Common Pleas of County	1
Alderman	1
Court of Quarter Sessions	1
Domestic Relations Court	1

TABLE 4

NUMBER OF STATES SPECIFYING DIFFERENT KINDS OF COURTS

NUMBER OF STATES	NUMBER OF COURTS
4	0
17	1
12	2
12	3
1	5
2	6

courts; no court is specified in four states, one court in seventeen states, two courts in twelve states and so on.

The designations of some of the courts are general rather than specific. There are four such general designations as "any court of competent jurisdiction"; "nearest court having jurisdiction"; "any court having jurisdiction of misdemeanors"; and "proper court." The justice of the peace, a local court, is specified by twenty states; it may be assumed, too, that many, if not all, of the above general designations include the justice of the peace. In that case, more than half of the states are committed to trying cases of compulsory education in the justice of the peace court. In addition, the police court, the city court, the recorder of the city, trial justice, magistrate, mayor, alderman, and possibly others are essentially local courts. The courts specified for a few of the states are not local. Such are county court, circuit court, district court, superior court, and recorder of the county.

In view of the criticisms which school administrators have made of enforcement by local officers, including courts, the specifying in so many states of local courts to try attendance cases, together with a lack of state and county supervision of the enforcement of the attendance laws, raises serious questions relative to the effectiveness of the enforcement of attendance laws.

PENALTIES IN COMPULSORY ATTENDANCE LAWS

The enforcement of laws defining misdemeanors depends on the imposition of penalties in cases where the provisions of the laws are violated. In attendance laws, the state legislatures determine what the provisions of the laws shall be and what the penalties shall be for violating those provisions. It is the function of the courts to determine when the laws have been violated, and in case of violation to fix the penalty within the limits set by the legislature.

The attendance laws specify a large number of persons who are subject to penalties for various offenses against compulsory education requirements. Twenty-eight classes of persons are designated. Three classes stand out with great frequency; namely, parents, employers, and children beyond the control of parents. Table 5 shows the classes of persons subject to penalty and the states in each case which definitely specify that class for penalty. Forty-six states expressly name parents as subject to penalty for the unlawful absence from school of chil-

TABLE 5

PERSONS SUBJECT TO PENALTIES IN STATE ATTENDANCE LAWS

States	Parents for Unlawful Absence	Employers for Unlawful Employment	Children Beyond Control	School Officers	Attendance Officers	Teachers in Public or Private Schools	Principals	City Superintendents	County Superintendents	District Supervisors	Members of Boards of Education	Persons Falsifying Regarding Child's Age	Persons Inducing Unlawful Absence	Clerks of Boards Failing to Make Census Reports	Persons Falsifying Census	Persons Evading Enumeration	Persons Hindering Enumeration	Clerks Falsifying about Enforcement of Attendance Laws	Secretaries Failing to Report Absences, or Children not Enrolled	Persons Falsifying Regarding Attendance	Persons Falsifying Age, Schooling or Work Certificate	Persons Instructing Children to Falsify about Age	Persons Withholding Information in Registration of Minors	Real Estate Dealers	Property Owners	Persons Interfering With Attendance Officers	Illiterate Minors Failing to Attend School	Parents of Insubordinate Children
Ala.....	x	x	x																									
Ariz....	x	x	x																									
Ark.....	x																											
Calif....	x	x	x																									
Colo....	x	x	x																									
Conn...	x	x	x									x										x						
Del.....	x		x																									
Fla.....	x		x						x																			
Ga.....	x	x																										
Idaho...	x	x	x											x														
Ill......	x	x	x																									
Ind.....	x	x	x																							x		
Iowa....	x	x																										
Kans....	x	x																										
Ky.....	x	x																										
La......	x	x	x																									
Me.....	x	x			x								x															
Md.....	x	x	x										x		x													
Mass....	x	x	x										x		x								x			x		
Mich....	x		x																									
Minn...	x	x	x	x	x	x	x	x	x				x															
Miss....	x		x																									
Mo.....	x	x	x												x													
Mont...	x	x												x														
Nebr....	x															x												
Nev....	x	x										x	x							x				x	x			
N. H....	x	x																										
N. J....	x	x	x																		x							
N. Mex.	x	x																										
N. Y....	x	x	x										x													x	x	x
N. C....	x																											
D. Dak..	x	x																										
Ohio....	x	x	x	x		x	x	x				x			x													
Okla....		x																										
Ore.....	x			x	x	x	x	x	x																			
Pa......	x	x	x			x	x	x	x								x		x							x		
R I....	x	x	x																									
S. C....	x	x																										
S. Dak..	x		x	x	x	x			x		x																	
Tenn...	x		x									x								x								
Tex.....	x	x	x																									x
Utah....			x																									
Vt......	x	x																										
Va......	x	x	x			x							x															
Wash...	x	x	x		x	x		x	x									x										
W. Va...	x	x		x	x	x	x	x	x	x			x															
Wis.....	x		x		x			x	x																			
Wyo....	x	x													x													

dren of school age under their control, and specify the penalties to be imposed. Only in the school laws of Oklahoma and Utah are no penalties specified. Utah makes it a misdemeanor for a parent to fail to comply with the attendance law, and other sections of the state law may specify the penalty. Thirty-six states specify employers as subject to penalty for the illegal employment of children of specified ages, and fix penalties. Twenty-nine states designate children who are beyond the control of their parents as subject to penalties by courts.

Table 6 shows the classes of persons subject to penalties

TABLE 6

PERSONS AND OFFENSES SUBJECT TO PENALTIES IN THE COMPULSORY ATTENDANCE LAWS

PERSONS	OFFENSES
1. Parents	Unlawful absence of children
2. Employers	Unlawful employment of children
3. School Officers	Failure to enforce attendance law
4. Attendance Officers	Failure to enforce attendance law
5. Teachers (Public and Private)	Failure to enforce attendance law
6. Principals	Failure to enforce attendance law
7. City Superintendents	Failure to enforce attendance law
8. County Superintendents	Failure to enforce attendance law
9. District Supervisors	Failure to enforce attendance law
10. Members of Boards of Education	Failure to enforce attendance law
11. Persons Inducing	Unlawful absence
12. Persons Falsifying	Census or enumeration
13. Persons Falsifying	Child's age
14. Persons Falsifying	Regarding attendance of child
15. Persons Falsifying	Age, schooling, or work certificate
16. Clerks of Boards	Failure to make census reports
17. Clerks Falsifying	Reports as to enforcement of attendance law
18. Secretaries Not Reporting	Absences or children not enrolled
19. Persons Withholding Information	In registration of minors
20. Persons Evading	Enumeration
21. Persons Hindering	Enumeration
22. Persons Instructing Children	To falsify about age
23. Real Estate Dealers	Failure to report change of residence
24. Property Owners	Failure to report change of residence
25. Persons Interfering	With attendance officers
26. Parents	Children insubordinate
27. Illiterate Minors	Failure to attend school
28. Children	Beyond control of parents

and the specific offense designated for each class. There are four large general groups of persons specified; namely, parents, employers, school officials, and persons falsifying, deceiving, or withholding information. A smaller group of persons interfering with attendance officers completes the list.

PENALTIES ON PARENTS

The laws provide two kinds of penalties on parents. They are money fines and imprisonment in jail. In fixing the limits and conditions of fines and imprisonments, the legislatures have left wide room for the discretion of the courts. Moreover, a great many of the legislatures have made no distinctions in fines and imprisonments in the case of recurring offenses. Whatever distinctions in penalty are made for the second or subsequent offenses are left to the discretion of the court. A smaller number of states specify in the law what distinctions the court shall make in cases of first, second, and subsequent offenses. Table 7 gives the ranges of fines and the respective states where no distinctions are made for recurring offenses. There are thirty-three states in this group. Here the court has wide discretion not only within the limits of each range, but as to the degree of penalty for second and subsequent offenses.

TABLE 7

RANGES OF FINES ON PARENTS IN ATTENDANCE LAWS WHERE THE LAW MAKES NO DISTINCTION AS TO RECURRING OFFENSES

RANGE	STATES
$10 to $200	Ind.
5 to 100	Nebr., N. Mex.
5 to 50	Ariz., Ala., Mich., Wis.
1 to 50	Ida., Minn.
10 to 25	Mo.
5 to 25	Iowa, Kans., N. C., Ore., Vt., Wyo.
1 to 25	Me., Va., Wash.
5 to 20	Colo., Ill., Mont., Ohio
3 to 20	W. Va.
1 to 20	Mass., R. I.
1 to 10	Ark., La.
5 to 10	S. C.
1 to 5	Conn., Md., Fla.
5 to no maximum specified	Ky.

In stating the ranges, where the law reads: "not more than five dollars," or "not more than ten dollars," the range is given the tables as "$1 to $5," or "$1 to $10."

A quotation from the Ohio law offers a typical statement of the provisions for penalties against parents.

> Whoever being a parent, guardian, or other person having care of a child of compulsory school age violates any of the provisions of (sections of the school law pertaining to compulsory attendance), shall upon conviction be fined not less than five dollars and not more than twenty dollars, or the court may in its discretion require the person so convicted to give bond in the sum of one hundred dollars with sureties to the approval of the court, conditioned that he will cause the child under his charge to attend upon instruction as provided by law, and remain as a pupil in the school or class during the term prescribed by law; and upon the failure or refusal of any such parent, guardian or other person to pay said fine and costs or furnish said bond according to the order of the court, the said parent, guardian or other person shall be imprisoned in the county jail not less than ten days nor more than thirty days.[1]

Besides the law of Ohio, the laws of Colorado, Montana, and New Hampshire provide for a bond which may be required at the discretion of the court.

The Indiana law provides for the most severe penalty by way of fine. It reads as follows:

> Any person, or any agent for any person or any minor who shall violate any of the provisions of Sections 1 to 17, inclusive, of this act, or who shall compel or encourage any minor to violate any of the provisions of Sections 1 to 17, inclusive, of this act, or any parent or guardian whose minor child or ward violates any provisions of Sections 1 to 17, inclusive, of this act, or any person who hinders or delays any officer or school official in the performance of his duty in the enforcement of this act, shall upon conviction be fined not less than ten dollars nor more than two hundred dollars; or be imprisoned in the county jail not exceeding sixty days, or both, such fine and imprisonment within the discretion of the court.[2]

At the other extreme from the Indiana law is the Maryland law which provides for the lowest minimum as well as the lowest maximum fine of the states reported in Table 7.

> Any person who has a child under his control and who fails to comply with any of the provisions of the preceding section shall be deemed guilty of a misdemeanor, and be fined not exceeding five dollars for each offense.[3]

[1] Ohio School Laws, 1922, p. 589.

[2] Indiana School Laws, 1923, p. 292.

[3] Maryland School Laws, 1922, p. 104.

In thirteen states, the law makes a distinction in fines for first offense, and second and subsequent offenses. By placing these distinctions in the law, legislatures limit somewhat the discretion of courts. In making these distinctions, legislatures indicate that they regard second and subsequent offenses as deserving of greater severity than the first offense.

Table 8 shows the ranges of fines for the first offense; Table 9 the ranges for the second offense for the same states. The fines in Tables 8 and 9 for Delaware, California, and Nevada do not overlap. The maximum for the first offense becomes the minimum for the second or subsequent offenses. The fines for South Dakota, North Dakota, Tennessee, Mississippi, New York, and Pennsylvania do overlap. For example, the maxi-

TABLE 8

Ranges of Fines on Parents in Attendance Laws for First Offense

Range	States
$10 to $50	S. Dak.
5 to 25	Del.
5 to 20	N. Dak.
10	Ga., N. H.
2 to 10	Tenn.
1 to 10	Calif., Miss., Mo.
5	N. J., Tex.
1 to 5	N. Y.
1 to 2	Pa.

TABLE 9

Ranges of Fines on Parents in Attendance Laws for Second Offense

Range	States
$25 to $100	S. Dak.(*a*)
25 to 50	Del.
10 to 50	N. Dak., Calif., Nev.
5 to 50	Tenn.(*a*)
1 to 50	N. Y.(*a*)
5 to 25	Miss.
1 to 25	N. J.(*a*)
20	Ga., N. H.
10	Texas
1 to 5	Pa.(*a*)

(*a*) = Second and subsequent offenses.

mum for the first offense in South Dakota is twenty-five dollars above the minimum for the second and subsequent offenses. In Table 9, it appears further that five of the states specify that the fine indicated is for the second and subsequent offenses.

In Mississippi, for all offenses after the second, the fine is not less than twenty-five dollars; in Texas for such offense after the second, it is twenty-five dollars.

If the ranges of fines in Tables 7, 8, and 9 are inspected, the wide variety of ranges becomes apparent. In order to compare Tables 8 and 9 with Table 7, the minimum of a range in Table 8 is placed with the maximum for the range of the same state in Table 9. This is done on the assumption that such a range establishes the extremes for those states for all offenses. The four states, Georgia, New Hampshire, New Jersey, and Texas, have no ranges but fix a definite fine in each table. They are not used in this comparison. The fixing of such a definite fine takes away much of the discretion that is placed with the court when limits are fixed within which a court may choose. The fixing of limits which give large discretion to the court is a recognition of the fact that violations of the compulsory attendance law by parents vary in the degree of gravity of the offense, and that the punishments imposed should be graded accordingly. To determine the gravity of each offense is a judicial function and the court should be given discretion to fix a fine commensurate with the gravity. Where a definite fine is established by the legislature, the only discretion left the court is that of imposing or not imposing the fine. It may be assumed that cases will be heard and determined by courts where a small fine might be justified, but where the court will impose no fine at all rather than the large one specified.

With Tables 8 and 9 rearranged and combined with Table 7, as suggested above, the ranges for all the states that have ranges are comparable. Table 10 shows what the combined ranges are and the states for each range. There are sixteen ranges for the forty-two states.

The ranges $5 to $50 and $5 to $25 apply to groups of six states each. The range $1 to $50 applies to five states. The ranges $1 to $25, $5 to $20, and $1 to $5 apply to groups of four states each. Table 10 represents a great variety of practice so far as the enactments of legislatures on this matter are concerned. The maximum in Indiana is forty times what it is in Connecticut, Florida, Maryland, and Pennsylvania. The maximum of South Dakota, Nebraska, and New Mexico is twenty times what it is for the same four states. It could not seriously be argued that the higher maximum represents a correspondingly higher value on the benefits of education or of a correspondingly greater determination to enforce the law. It seems quite probable that the degree of enforcement of a law by the courts will be affected by the penalties provided. Since

TABLE 10

RANGES OF FINES ON PARENTS IN ATTENDANCE LAWS IN ALL STATES COMPARED

Range	States
$10 to $200	Ind.
10 to 100	S. Dak.
5 to 100	Nebr., N. Mex.
5 to 50	Ariz., Ala., Del., Mich., N. Dak., Wis.
2 to 50	Tenn.
1 to 50	Calif., Ida., Minn., Nev., N. Y.
10 to 25	Mo.
5 to 25	Iowa, Kans., N. C., Ore., Vt., Wyo.
1 to 25	Miss., Me., Va., Wash.
5 to 20	Colo., Ill., Mont., Ohio
3 to 20	W. Va.
1 to 20	Mass., R. I.
1 to 10	Ark., La.
5 to 10	S. C.
1 to 5	Conn., Fla., Md., Pa.
5 to no maximum specified	Ky.

the degree with which the maximum is approached lies within the discretion of the court, the maximum probably does not affect court action to the extent that the various minima do. For example, the minimum for Indiana, South Dakota, and Missouri is as great as, or greater than, the maximum for Arkansas, Louisiana, South Carolina, Connecticut, Florida, Maryland, and Pennsylvania. If a rather high minimum like ten dollars led to a hesitation on the part of school officials to bring charges, or in case charges were brought, to an indisposition on the part of courts to impose the penalty, the question might seriously be raised as to whether the fine was not a hindrance rather than a help to enforce the law. A high minimum obviously limits the discretion of the court. Considering the minima in Table 10, it is seen that twenty-two states have a minimum of five dollars or more. Nineteen have a minimum of less than five dollars. Data are not available for determining the effect of such widely varying fines on court action in all the states involved.

In Table 11, the ranges of imprisonment for parents are shown. As in the case of the fines, the wide ranges indicate that much discretion is given courts in determining the amount of imprisonment to be imposed. Wide variations in the maxima and minima of different states are observed here as in the fines. Noticeable is the fact that in the case of nine states in this table, the minimum imprisonment is five days or more. The

TABLE 11

RANGES OF IMPRISONMENT FOR PARENTS IN ATTENDANCE LAWS IN ALL STATES COMPARED

RANGE	STATES
5 to 90 days	N. Mex.
2 to 90 days	Mich.
1 to 90 days	Nebr., Wis., Wyo.
1 to 60 days	Ind.
10 to 30 days	Colo.(c), Mont.(c), Ohio(c), S. Dak.(b)
1 to 30 days	Ala., Minn., Me., N. Y.(b), N. C.(g)
25 days	Ariz.
5 to 25 days	Calif.(b), Nev.(b)
5 to 20 days	W. Va.
10 days	Miss.(f)
5 to 10 days	S. C.
2 to 10 days	Mo., Ore.
1 to 10 days	La.
5 days	Del.(e)
1 to 5 days	Calif.(a), Fla.(c), Nev.(a), N. Y.(a), Pa.(g)
2 days	Del.(d)

(a) = First offense.
(b) = Second and subsequent offenses.
(c) = On refusal or failure to pay fine or give bond.
(d) = On default of fine for first offense.
(e) = On default of fine for second and subsequent offenses.
(f) = Third and succeeding offenses.
(g) = On refusal or failure to pay fine.

same doubt may be expressed in the case of such penalties, as in the case of the fines, as to whether they will not operate to prevent enforcement rather than to further it. It seems reasonable to infer that where a court has no other choice in the matter of imprisonment than to sentence a parent to jail for five days or ten days, serious consideration will be given to finding some other way out. Instead of a jail sentence of such severity, a lecture or a suspended sentence may be substituted. In the interest of facilitating enforcement, legislatures should legalize punishments that are likely to be imposed.

The Illinois and Kansas laws provide for imprisonment until the fine is paid. In addition to fine and imprisonment, the New Mexico law provides for a writ of mandamus against an offending parent. The following fifteen states provide for fines but in the school laws consulted have not specified imprisonment under any conditions: Connecticut, Georgia, Iowa, Kentucky, Maryland, Massachusetts, North Dakota, New Hampshire, New Jersey, Rhode Island, Tennessee, Texas, Vermont, Virginia, and Washington.

Table 12 shows a wide variation in the maximum limits of imprisonment and gives the number of states for each maximum. The highest maximum is ninety days; the lowest maximum is two days. The mode is thirty days.

TABLE 12

MAXIMUM LIMITS OF IMPRISONMENT IN ATTENDANCE LAWS

DAYS	NUMBER OF STATES
90	5
60	1
30	9
25	3
20	1
10	5
5	6
2	1

Since many state laws provide a penalty of a fine and an alternative prison sentence, it is desirable to know the relationship between the two. This is shown in Table 13. Here are shown twenty-seven ranges of fines in dollars and their corresponding prison sentences in ranges of days. In only two cases are there as many as two states having the same range of fines and the same range of days in prison. The relationship between each range of fines and its corresponding range of days in prison is not always clear. In a few cases like Florida, New York, Louisiana, Pennsylvania, and South Carolina there is a clear relationship. One dollar of fine in those states is meant to be equivalent to a day in prison. In some states, the maximum prison sentence is greater in days than the maximum fine in dollars, as in Colorado, Montana, Michigan, Maine, North Caro-

TABLE 13

RELATION OF FINES IN ATTENDANCE LAWS TO ALTERNATIVE PRISON SENTENCES

FINE	PRISON SENTENCE	STATE
$ 5 to $ 50	1 to 25 days	Ariz.
5 to 50	1 to 30 days	Ala.
1 to 10	1 to 5 days	Calif.(*a*)
10 to 50	5 to 25 days	Calif.(*b*)
5 to 20	10 to 30 days	Colo.
5 to 25	2 days	Del.(*a*)
25 to 50	5 days	Del.(*c*)
1 to 5	1 to 5 days	Fla., N. Y.(*a*)
10 to 200	1 to 60 days	Ind.
1 to 10	1 to 10 days	La.
5 to 20	10 to 30 days	Mont.
10 to 25	2 to 10 days	Mo.
5 to 50	2 to 90 days	Mich.
1 to 50	1 to 30 days	Minn., N. Y.(*c*)
1 to 25	1 to 30 days	Me.
5 to 100	1 to 90 days	Nebr.
1 to 10	1 to 5 days	Nev.(*a*)
10 to 50	5 to 25 days	Nev.(*c*)
5 to 100	5 to 90 days	N. Mex.
5 to 25	1 to 30 days	N. C.
5 to 25	2 to 10 days	Ore.
1 to 5(*b*)	1 to 5(*b*) days	Pa.
5 to 10	5 to 10 days	S. C.
25 to 100(*c*)	10 to 30(*c*) days	S. Dak.
3 to 20	5 to 20 days	W. Va.
5 to 50	1 to 90 days	Wis
5 to 25	1 to 90 days	Wyo.

(*a*) = First offense.
(*b*) = Second offense.
(*c*) = Offenses subsequent to first.

lina, Wisconsin, and Wyoming. In other states, the opposite is true as in Arizona, Alabama, California, Delaware, Indiana, Missouri, Minnesota, New York, Nebraska, Nevada, New Mexico, Oregon, and South Dakota.

PENALTIES ON EMPLOYERS

As shown in Table 5, there are thirty-six states that provide expressly in their school laws for the punishment of employers who unlawfully employ children of school age. It has been pointed out that compelling attendance of children at school and preventing their employment are complementary features in the attainment of the same purpose.[4] The legislatures of the states have made it a misdemeanor, punishable by fine and imprisonment, for parents to be responsible for the unlawful absence of their children of school age from school. At the same time, they have made it a misdemeanor, punishable by fine and imprisonment, for employers to be responsible for employing such children unlawfully in their establishments. The complementary relationship of the attendance of children at school to their freedom from labor is well stated in the Ohio law. It defines certain violators of law and fixes a penalty in these words:

> Whoever being an officer or agent of a corporation, participates or acquiesces in any violation of law relating to compulsory education or employment of minors shall upon conviction be fined not less than twenty dollars, nor more than fifty dollars.[5]

Table 14 shows the ranges of fines on employers in the various state laws, and the state or states for each range. Twenty-nine different fines are indicated, including the differentiations in a few states for second and third offenses. The ranges vary from "$1 to $500" in Missouri to "$1 to $10" in Louisiana and Rhode Island. In other words, a fine may be fifty times as great in Missouri, or thirty times as great in Arizona, as in Louisiana and Rhode Island. With the exception of Massachusetts, Nevada, Georgia, and Texas, which fix one definite fine, the legislatures have left in the ranges provided wide room for the use of discretion by the courts. Kentucky specifies a minimum fine of five dollars but specifies no maximum. This

[4] Ensign, F. C. *Compulsory School Attendance and Child Labor*, p. 3.
[5] Ohio School Laws, 1922, p. 590.

is evidently a defect in legislation. To require the court to fix a maximum is probably extending the field of discretion too far.

TABLE 14

RANGES OF FINES ON EMPLOYERS IN ATTENDANCE LAWS

RANGE	STATES
$100 to $500	Ala.(*b*)
30 to 500	Ohio(*d*)
1 to 500	Mo.
10 to 300	Ariz.
1 to 250	Ind.(*d*)
50 to 200	Calif., Mass.(*b*)
25 to 200	Me.
20 to 200	Ohio(*c*)
10 to 200	Pa.
5 to 200	Vt.
1 to 200	N. Y.(*b*)
50 to 100	Ind.(*c*)
25 to 100	Colo., Wyo.
10 to 100	Ala.(*a*)
50	Nev.
25 to 50	W. Va., Ind.(*a*), Mont.
20 to 50	N. Dak.
10 to 50	Mass.(*a*), Ohio(*a*), Okla.
5 to 50	N. Mex.
1 to 50	Ida., N.H., Md., Minn., N.Y.(*a*)
5 to 25	Iowa, Kans.
1 to 25	N. J., Wash., Va.
20	Ga.(*b*)
5 to 20	Ill.
1 to 20	Conn.
10	Ga.(*a*), Tex.
5 to 10	S. C.
1 to 10	La., R. I.
5 to no maximum specified	Ky.

(*a*) = First offense.
(*b*) = Offenses subsequent to first.
(*c*) = Second offense.
(*d*) = Third and subsequent offenses.

Sixteen states provide for imprisonment as a feature of the penalty to which employers may be subject. What the limits in days are for these imprisonments is shown in Table 15. As in the fines, great variations among the states are indicated, as well as wide discretion for courts within the states. Three of these states provide no prison sentence for the first offense. One of these three, Indiana, provides different prison sentences for the second and the third offenses, and provides further that these prison sentences are not an alternative for the fine but may be added to the fine in the discretion of the court. Kansas and Illinois provide that the convicted person shall be committed to prison until the fine is paid. Fifteen of the states that provide for a fine on employers make no specific provision for imprisonment. These states are: Alabama, Colorado, Connecticut, Georgia, Idaho, Kentucky, Maryland, Maine, Montana, New Mexico, New Hampshire, North Dakota, Rhode Island, Texas, and Washington.

TABLE 15

RANGES OF IMPRISONMENT FOR EMPLOYERS IN ATTENDANCE LAWS

RANGE	STATES
1 to 180 days	Mo., Vt.(*a*)
30 to 90 days	Wyo.
1 to 90 days	Ariz.
1 to 60 days	Calif., Mass.(*a*)
10 to 30 days	Okla.
5 to 30 days	W. Va.
1 to 30 days	Mass., Minn., N. J., Ind.(*c*)
25 days	Nev.
5 to 10 days	S. C.
1 to 10 days	La., N. Y., Pa., Ind.(*b*)

(*a*) = Offenses subsequent to first.
(*b*) = Second offense.
(*c*) = Third offense.

In Table 16, the relation between the fine in a state and the alternative prison sentence of that state is shown. South Carolina and Louisiana have the relation of one dollar in fine being equivalent to one day of imprisonment. In Nevada, a day in prison is equivalent to two dollars in fine. In Pennsylvania, a day in prison ranges from ten to twenty dollars in fine. In most of the states, it does not appear that the legislature had any definite relationship in view. The adjusting of fine to prison sentence is left to the discretion of the court. In general, the maximum fines are higher than the corresponding maximum prison sentences. This is true in all cases except Arizona, New Jersey, South Carolina, and Louisiana.

The legislation fixing the severe penalties which courts are authorized to impose on employers indicates a vast change in public sentiment towards child labor since 1868, when an attempt was being made in Massachusetts to enforce laws regarding the employment of children.[6] The enforcing officer at that time found the most serious defects to enforcement to be:

1. No power to secure evidence of violation.
2. No power to enter and inspect places of employment.
3. No specific provision for court jurisdiction nor for manner of prosecution.
4. No form of age and schooling certificate to be kept on file by the employer.

Employers, moreover, took the stand that "the state was meddling with what it had no right to interfere with, and was making unjustifiable investigations into the private business of corporations."

TABLE 16

RELATION OF FINES ON EMPLOYERS IN ATTENDANCE LAWS TO ALTERNATIVE PRISON SENTENCES

FINE	PRISON SENTENCE	STATE
$30 to $500	1 to 60 days	Ohio (*b*)
1 to 500	1 to 180 days	Mo.
50 to 200	1 to 60 days	Calif.
20 to 200	1 to 30 days	Ohio(*a*)
10 to 200	1 to 10 days	Pa.
25 to 100	30 to 90 days	Wyo.
50	25 days	Nev.
25 to 50	5 to 30 days	W. Va.
10 to 50	10 to 30 days	Okla.
1 to 50	1 to 30 days	Minn.
1 to 50	1 to 10 days	N. Y.
10 to 30	1 to 90 days	Ariz.
1 to 25	1 to 30 days	N. J.
5 to 10	5 to 10 days	S. C.
1 to 10	1 to 10 days	La.

(*a*) = Second offense.
(*b*) = Third and subsequent offenses.

[6] Ensign, F. C. *Compulsory School Attendance and Child Labor*, p. 59.

The present Massachusetts law affecting the employment of children is an excellent illustration of legislation which provides every necessary safeguard to insure children that freedom from employment which is precedent to attendance at school. After specifying in a number of sections the prohibitions at labor of children at different ages and under defined conditions, the law fixes penalties as follows:

> Whoever by himself or for others, or through agents, servants, or foremen, employs, induces, or permits any minor to work contrary to any provision of sections sixty to seventy-four, inclusive, shall, except as provided in section sixty-one, be punished for a first offense by a fine of not less than ten nor more than fifty dollars or by imprisonment for not more than one month, or both, and for a subsequent offense by a fine of not less than fifty nor more than two hundred dollars or by imprisonment for not more than two months, or both. The employment of any minor in violation of any provision of said sections, after the person employing such minor has been notified thereof in writing by any authorized inspector or school attendance officer, shall constitute a separate offense for every day, during which the employment continues.[7]

The next section provides that

> Any person who hinders or delays any authorized inspector or school attendance officer in the performance of his duties, or who refuses to admit to or locks out any such inspector or officer from any place which such inspector or officer is authorized to inspect, or who refuses to give such inspector or officer such information as may be required for the proper enforcement of sections sixty to seventy-four, inclusive, shall be punished by a fine of not less than twenty-five nor more than two hundred dollars or by imprisonment for not more than two months, or both.[8]

Another section provides penalties of fines and imprisonment for parents or guardians who certify to any false statement for the purpose of obtaining illegal employment for a minor child. And still another section provides penalties for inspectors, school attendance officers, superintendents of schools, and other persons charged with the enforcement of provisions of the child labor law, who fail to comply with provisions of enforcement. In addition, minors who engage in illegal employment are subject to penalty also.[9] Thus the child, the parent, the employer, and all officials on whom the law imposes a duty for enforcing child labor enactments are liable to severe punishments for violations of these enactments. There is no doubt

[7] Massachusetts School Laws, 1921, p. 115.
[8] *Ibid.*, p. 115. [9] *Ibid.*, p. 116.

that society in Massachusetts is determined to protect the time of minors for school purposes by convicting and punishing in court those who are guilty of using that time unlawfully.

COMPARISON OF PENALTIES ON EMPLOYERS AND ON PARENTS

A study of the penalties provided in legislation for the offenses of employers and of parents discloses that legislatures have made distinctions in most cases as to the gravity of the two kinds of offenses. Table 17 shows the thirty-two states

TABLE 17

RELATIONS OF FINES ON EMPLOYERS AND ON PARENTS IN ATTENDANCE LAWS

EMPLOYERS	PARENTS	STATE
$10 to $300	$ 5 to $ 50	Ariz.
10 to 100	5 to 50	Ala.
25 to 100	5 to 20	Colo.
50 to 200	1 to 10	Calif.
1 to 20	1 to 5	Conn.
20	10	Ga.
25 to 50	10 to 200	Ind.
1 to 50	1 to 50	Ida.
5 to 25	5 to 25	Iowa
5 to 20	5 to 20	Ill.
5 to 25	5 to 25	Kans.
5	5	Ky.
1 to 10	1 to 10	La.
1 to 50	1 to 50	Minn.
1 to 500	10 to 25	Mo.
25 to 50	5 to 20	Mont.
1 to 50	1 to 5	Md.
10 to 50	1 to 20	Mass.
5 to 50	5 to 100	N. Mex.
20 to 50	5 to 20	N. Dak.
1 to 50	10	N. H.
50	1 to 10	Nev.
1 to 25	5	N. J.
1 to 50	1 to 5	N. Y.
10 to 50	5 to 20	Ohio
10 to 200	1 to 2	Pa.
1 to 10	1 to 20	R. I.
5 to 10	5 to 10	S. C.
10	5	Tex.
5 to 200	5 to 25	Vt.
1 to 25	1 to 25	Wash.
25 to 100	5 to 25	Wyo.

which have fines or ranges of fines specified for both employers and parents, and names the specific fines in each case. In nine states, namely, Idaho, Iowa, Illinois, Kansas, Kentucky, Louisiana, Minnesota, South Carolina, and Washington, the fines are the same for both kinds of offenses. In three states, Indiana, New Mexico, and Rhode Island, the provisions for fines on the employer are less than on the parent. In twenty states, namely, Arizona, Alabama, Colorado, California, Connecticut, Georgia, Missouri, Montana, Maryland, Massachusetts, North Dakota, New Hampshire, Nevada, New Jersey, New York, Ohio, Pennsylvania, Texas, Vermont, and Wyoming, the provisions for fines on the employer are greater than on the parent. In general, therefore, so far as legislation is concerned, the offenses of employers are regarded as more grave than the offenses of parents.

This fact is made clearer still in Tables 18 and 19, where the relations of the maximum and minimum fines are shown. In Table 18, the maximum for employers in nineteen states is fifty dollars or above; in only six states is the maximum for parents fifty dollars or above. In Table 19 the minimum for employers in eleven states is ten dollars or above; for parents, the highest minimum of ten dollars is fixed in only two states. In connection with these relatively severe penalties against employers it is well to recall the fact that in the study of court decisions only one case was found involving child labor and compulsory attendance. Apparently employers have not regarded it as profitable to employ children illegally and run the risks of the penalties involved.

TABLE 18

Relations of Maximum Fines on Employers and on Parents in Attendance Laws

Employers		Parents	
Fine	Number of States	Fine	Number of States
$500	1	$200	1
300	1	100	1
200	3	50	4
100	3	25	6
50	11	20	7
25	4	10	4
20	2	5	3
10	3	2	1

TABLE 19

RELATIONS OF MAXIMUM FINES ON EMPLOYERS AND ON PARENTS IN ATTENDANCE LAWS

Employers		Parents	
Fine	Number of States	Fine	Number of States
$50	1	$10	2
25	4	5	13
20	1	1	12
10	5		
5	6		
1	11		

PENALTIES ON SCHOOL OFFICIALS

As already shown, the two largest groups for whom offenses punishable by fines and imprisonment are defined in state legislation concerning school attendance are parents and employers. The next considerable group as indicated in Table 5 and Table 6 are school officials. Items 3 to 10 inclusive in Table 6 list the titles by which these officials are designated in the state laws. For the offenses defined, these officials are subject to being tried by a court, and if convicted shall have imposed by the court a penalty determined by the legislature. These officials include what may be called the enforcing officers for the attendance laws. If cases are brought to the courts for adjudication, they will be brought largely on the initiative of these officials. The information on which the courts base their dispositions of cases will be furnished largely by these officials. The offenses of these officials as defined in the law consist in general of a failure to enforce the attendance laws. The efficient functioning of the courts depends on the degree of efficiency with which these officials perform their part of the duty of enforcing attendance laws.

In view of the importance of their positions, it is pertinent to observe to what extent the state laws recognize these officials by defining their failure to perform their duties as an offense for which conviction in court will bring a specified punishment. An inspection of Table 5 shows that mention of these officials is limited to a few states, and that not all of the states make mention of all these officials. Table 20 shows the states in which one or more of these officials is mentioned in the law, and the penalty designated for the offense defined. The term "school officers" in this list of officials is a general term that is doubtless meant to include the other officials in most cases. Maine, Virginia, and Florida each mention one official or type of official. The states mentioning the largest number are Minnesota, Oregon, and West Virginia, each of which mentions six.

The Minnesota law defines the offense and the punishment for it in the cases of these school officials as follows:

> Any school officer, truant officer, teacher of a public or private school, graded school principal, city superintendent or county superintendent of schools refusing, willfully failing, or neglecting to perform any duty imposed upon him by the provisions of this act shall be guilty of a misdemeanor, and upon conviction shall be punished for each offense by a fine not to exceed ten dollars ($10), or by imprisonment in the county jail not to exceed ten (10) days.[10]

The Minnesota school law in other sections defines at length and in detail the duties of school board, county superintendent,

TABLE 20

School Officials in Attendance Laws Subject to Penalties

States	School Officers	Attendance Officers	Teachers	Principals	City Superintendents	County Superintendents	District Supervisor	Members of Boards of Education	Total Number of States
Me. . . .		$10-50							1
Minn. .	$10	10	$10	$10	$10	$10			6
Ohio . .	20-50		20-50	20-50	20-50				4
Ore. . . .	5-20	5-20	5-20	5-20	5-20	5-20			6
Pa. . . .			1-25	1-25	1-25	1-25			4
S. Dak.		10-50(*a*) 25-100(*b*)	10-50(*a*) 25-100(*b*)			10-50(*a*) 25-100(*b*)		$10-50(*a*) 25-100(*b*)	4
Wash. .		20-100	20-100		20-100	20-100			4
W. Va. .	3-20		3-20	3-20	3-20	3-20	$3.20		6
Wis. . .		5-25	5-25		5-25	5-25			4
Va. . . .	5-50								1
Fla. . . .						1-50			1
Total . .	5	6	8	5	7	8	1	1	

(*a*) = First offense
(*b*) = Offenses subsequent to first

[10] Minnesota School Laws, 1923, p. 81.

teacher, city superintendent, principal, and attendance officer. These officials have duties imposed by the state law and are held accountable to be punished for a failure to perform their duties. Thus the state sets up standards of enforcement and fixes responsibility for enforcement in such a way that there can be no evasion of duties by local officials on the grounds that they do not know what the duties of enforcement are or who is to perform them.

In Table 20 only the penalty of a fine is indicated. Forty-one cases of fine are shown in the chart; in twenty of these cases the law provides a prison sentence as well as a fine. It is noticeable that where a state specifies a penalty for several of the officials, the same fine is specified in each case. This is probably the legislature's way of indicating that the different officials named were equally responsible for performing their duties in enforcing the attendance law.

PENALTIES ON PERSONS FALSIFYING, DECEIVING, OR WITHHOLDING INFORMATION

Legislatures have defined some punishable offenses for adjudication by the courts in furthering the enforcement of attendance laws, which may be classified under the concepts of falsifying, deceiving, or withholding information. In Table 6, items 11 to 24 inclusive comprise in one group the classes of persons of this kind and their specific offenses. In enforcing attendance laws, enforcement officers and courts meet with cases involving falsification, deception, and evasion. In the matter of rendering judgments in controverted cases, courts, in order to dispense justice, must have reliable information. If parties, who are responsible under the law for giving items of information or for assembling a body of information necessary for the proper enforcement of the attendance laws, may falsify, deceive, or evade with impunity, it will be impossible to enforce the law adequately and to dispense justice. Legislation defining offenses of this kind and fixing penalties commensurate with the gravity of the offense is a recognition of the primary importance of the facts, or of the truth, as a basis for the functioning both of school officials and of courts.

Table 21 gives the group of fourteen classes of persons of this kind, the offense for which they are subject to conviction and penalty by the court, and the states in which each class is defined as an offense. The class on which the largest number of states has legislated is with reference to persons who induce children to absent themselves unlawfully from school. This class is included in this group on the ground that the offense

TABLE 21

STATES SPECIFYING IN ATTENDANCE LAWS OFFENSES FOR FALSIFYING, DECEIVING, OR WITHHOLDING INFORMATION

OFFENSE	STATES
1. Persons Inducing Unlawful Absence...	Md., Me., Mass., Minn., Nev., N. Y., Va., W. Va.
2. Persons Falsifying Census or Enumeration	Md., Mass., Mo., Ohio, Wyo.
3. Persons Falsifying Child's Age	Conn., Nev., Ohio, Tenn.
4. Persons Falsifying Regarding Attendance of Child	Nev., Tenn.
5. Persons Falsifying Regarding Age, Schooling, and Work Certificates	N. J.
6. Clerks of Boards Failing to Make Census Reports	Ida., Mont.
7. Clerks of Boards Falsifying Reports about Enforcement of Attendance Law	Wash.
8. Secretaries not Reporting Absence or Children not Enrolled	Pa.
9. Persons Withholding Information in Registration	Mass.
10. Persons Evading Enumeration	Nebr.
11. Persons Hindering Enumeration	Pa.
12. Persons Instructing Children to Falsify about Age	Conn.
13. Real Estate Dealers Failing to Report Change of Residence	Nev.
14. Property Owners Failing to Report Change of Residence	Nev.

may be a form of deception on children, parents, and school. Since each of the states that have made this an offense has also defined offenses for parents and employers in violating the attendance law, it seems reasonable to conclude that the persons committing this offense are, in some cases, neither parents nor employers.

The legislatures are safeguarding the time of children not only from parents and employers but also from persons who are neither parent nor employer to the children concerned, but who are at the same time influencing them to stay out of school. This represents an extension of the restraint of the law to an additional class of persons. No doubt, experience is showing that some children are induced to stay away from school and that the responsibility for such influence is greater on some one else than a parent or an employer.

Table 22 shows the ranges of fines for persons inducing unlawful absence. Eight state legislatures have considered such a thing as serious enough to define it as a punishable offense. The maximum fines enacted may be regarded as a measure of seriousness. Five of these states have a range of fines for this offense from "$1 to $50."

TABLE 22

RANGES OF FINES IN ATTENDANCE LAWS FOR PERSONS INDUCING ABSENCE

RANGE	STATE
$ 1 to $50	Mass.
1 to 50	Minn.
20	Me.
1 to 50	Nev.
1 to 50	N. Y.
25 to 50	W. Va.
1 to 50	Md.
1 to 25	Va.

The Massachusetts law is a typical expression of the definition of this offense:

> Any person who induces or attempts to induce any child to absent himself unlawfully from school, or unlawfully employs him or harbors a minor who, while school is in session, is absent unlawfully therefrom, shall be punished by a fine of not more than fifty dollars.[11]

The validity of the census or enumeration of children of school age is protected in a positive manner in five states, as shown in Table 21. The Ohio law on the false enumeration of school children indicates the gravity of the offense in that state:

[11] Massachusetts School Laws, 1921, p. 74.

Whoever being an officer or appointee responsible for securing or reporting the annual enumeration of children makes a false return shall upon conviction be fined not less than twenty nor more than one thousand dollars or imprisoned not less than ten days nor more than thirty days.[12]

This is the severest penalty provided in the five states. In Maryland, the fine is not more than twenty dollars; in Massachusetts not more than fifty dollars; in Missouri not more than one hundred dollars; in Wyoming from ten to one hundred.

Four states define as a punishable offense the falsification of a child's age. The provisions of the Connecticut law are:

Every parent or other person having control of a child, who shall make any false statement concerning the age of such child with intent to deceive the town clerk or registrar of births, marriages, and deaths of any town, or the teacher of any school, or shall instruct a child to make any such false statement, shall be fined not more than twenty dollars.[13]

The penalty in Nevada is a fine of fifty dollars or imprisonment twenty-five days or both; in Tennessee a fine from five to twenty dollars; in Ohio a fine from twenty to fifty dollars, or imprisonment one to thirty days.

Table 23 shows the ranges of fines for the classes of offenses numbered 4 to 14 inclusive in Table 21. As a case of severe penalty, class No. 5, New Jersey, imposing a penalty for falsi-

TABLE 23

FINES FOR CLASSES 4 TO 14 IN TABLE 21

CLASS NO.	STATE	FINE
4	Nev.	$ 1 to $ 50
4	Tenn.	5 to 20
5	N. J.	1 to 100
6	Ida.	5 to 50
6	Mont.	10 to 50
7	Wash.	25 to 100
8	Pa.	1 to 25
9	Mass.	1 to 50
10	Nebr.	10 to 50
11	Pa.	5 to 25
12	Conn.	1 to 20
13	Nev.	1 to 50
14	Nev.	1 to 50

[12] Ohio School Laws, 1922, p. 587.
[13] Connecticut School Laws, 1922, p. 15.

fying regarding age, schooling, and work certificates attracts attention. The provision of this law is as follows:

> All oaths, affirmations, and affidavits required to be made or taken in any proceeding had pursuant to this act in an application for an age and schooling certificate or age and working certificate shall be taken by the supervisor of school exemption certificates, and the said supervisor of school exemption certificates is hereby granted the power to administer oaths and take affidavits and affirmation in all such proceedings held pursuant to this act. Any person who shall swear or affirm falsely at any hearing or any proceeding taken pursuant to this act to an application for an age and schooling certificate or age and working certificate, or shall sign and swear or affirm to any affidavit containing a false statement to be used in any such proceeding, shall be guilty of committing perjury and, upon conviction thereof, shall be fined not exceeding one thousand dollars or imprisoned with or without hard labor as the court may direct for any time not to exceed three years, or both.[14]

It is evident that falsification in this law is regarded as a very serious offense. In New Jersey violations by parents and by employers of the law affecting attendance of children at school are far less grave than the falsifications as defined.

OTHER CLASSES OF OFFENSES PENALIZED

Table 5 shows that four states specify penalties of fine and imprisonment for persons who interfere with attendance officers. The New York law, after specifying the duties of attendance officers and the conditions under which they may arrest truants, has the following provision:

> Any person interfering with an attendance officer in the lawful discharge of his duties and any person owning and operating a factory, mercantile or other establishment, who shall refuse on demand to exhibit to such attendance officer the registry of the children employed or the employment certificate of such children shall be guilty of a misdemeanor.[15]

For this offense, Massachusetts has a penalty of a fine of from twenty-five to two hundred dollars or imprisonment one to sixty days, or both; Indiana a fine of from ten to two hundred dollars, or imprisonment one to sixty days, or both; and Pennsylvania a fine of five to twenty-five dollars and in default of payment imprisonment not exceeding thirty days.

The states of New York and Texas provide for penalizing

[14] New Jersey School Laws, 1921, pp. 114, 115.

[15] New York School Laws, 1923, p. 210.

the parents of children that are insubordinate. The Texas law provides as follows:

> Any child within the compulsory school ages, who shall be insubordinate, disorderly, vicious, or immoral in conduct, or who persistently violates the reasonable rules and regulations of the school which he attends, or who otherwise persistently misbehaves therein so as to render himself an incorrigible, shall be reported to the person exercising the duties of attendance officer of said school, who shall proceed against such child in the juvenile court as herein provided. If such child is found guilty upon a charge or charges made against him in said court, the judge of said court shall have the power to parole said child, after requiring the parent or other person standing in parental relation to execute a bond in the sum of not less than ten dollars, conditioned that said child shall attend school regularly and comply with all the rules and regulations of said school. . . . If said child shall be found guilty of violating the conditions of said parole, the bond provided for herein shall forthwith be declared forfeited.[16]

The New York education law provides a penalty for illiterate minors. The illiterate minor is defined as well as the requirements as to his attendance. This penalty is then fixed:

> Any minor subject to the provisions of this section, who wilfully violates any provisions of this section, shall be punished by a fine of not exceeding five dollars.[17]

For the same offense, the South Dakota law has a penalty of a fine of from twenty-five to one hundred dollars, or imprisonment from ten to thirty days, or both, in the discretion of the court.

PENALTIES ON CHILDREN BEYOND CONTROL OF PARENTS

There is one class of persons in cases heard under the compulsory attendance laws, whose penalties in the courts are not fines and imprisonments in jail. This class consists of children of school age who are beyond the control of the parents. So long as a child is adjudged under the control of the parent, the parent is punished for any violation of the compulsory attendance law by the child. If a child is adjudged beyond the control of the parent, the parent is relieved of accountability to the law, and the court imposes punishment on the child.

Most of the states make express provision in accordance with

[16] Texas School Laws, 1924, p. 145.
[17] New York School Laws, 1923, p. 213.

which a court hears and disposes of cases involving such children. The laws define in specific terms the offense of a child that refuses to attend school and is beyond the parent's control. Table 24 shows what the different terms for the offense are. In this chart, fifteen different terms are used. The most common one is "delinquent child," being used eight times. "Habitual truant" is used three times; "juvenile disorderly per-

TABLE 24

STATES, TERMS FOR OFFENSES, AND DISPOSITIONS OF CASES OF CHILDREN BEYOND CONTROL OF PARENTS

STATE	TERM FOR THE OFFENSE	DISPOSITION
Ala.	Incorrigibility	May be sentenced to a state school.
Ariz.	Delinquency	May be placed in a public or private home, or other institution where schooling may be provided, or otherwise.
Calif.	Habitual truant	Shall be committed to a parental school.
Colo.	Juvenile disorderly person	Shall be committed to a children's home, or to an industrial or training school.
Conn.	Vagrant child	May be committed to any institution of instruction or correction, or house of reformation, or, if a boy not less than ten, to the Connecticut School for Boys.
Del.	Disorderly pupil	May be sentenced to a state school.
Fla.	Child beyond parental control	Shall be committed to state school or other correctional school.
Ind.	Confirmed truant	May be sentenced to a state school, or some other custodial institution or to the care of a probation officer.
Idaho	Juvenile disorderly person	Shall be committed to a children's home, or to the Idaho Industrial Training School, or to some other training school.
Ill.	Delinquent child	Shall be committed to parental school.
La.	Delinquent child	May be placed in a home, public or private institution, or otherwise.
Miss.	Disorderly person	May be sentenced to any custodial institution, and if no school institution be available, be expelled from school.

TABLE 24 (*Continued*)

STATES, TERMS FOR OFFENSES, AND DISPOSITIONS OF CASES OF CHILDREN BEYOND CONTROL OF PARENTS

STATE	TERM FOR THE OFFENSE	DISPOSITION
Md.	Incorrigible truant	Shall be committed to a parental school, or some other suitable institution.
Mass.	Habitual truant	May be committed to a county training school, or paroled under attendance officer or probation officer. The court may commit inmates of training schools for gross misbehavior to a state school.
Mo.	Delinquent child	May be committed to parental school.
Minn.	Delinquent child	May be committed to ungraded or truant school.
N. J.	Juvenile delinquent	Shall abide by the action of the court.
N. Y.	Disorderly person	Confined in truant school, private school, orphans' home, or other similar institution.
Ohio	Delinquent or dependent child	Court shall determine and dispose of case.
Pa.	Incorrigibility, truancy, insubordination	Shall be proceeded against in court by school officials.
R. I.	Delinquent child	May order child paroled to probation officer, or parent, or may commit child to a state detention home.
S. Dak.	Delinquent child	Action shall be instituted against him in proper court by those charged with enforcing attendance law.
Tex.	Habitual truant	Shall be committed to school agreed upon between parent and judge.
Tenn.	Delinquent child	Parent shall be discharged from liability, and child be proceeded against.
Utah	Incorrigible child	Shall be committed to state industrial school.
Va.	Delinquent child	Shall be proceeded against in a tribunal of competent jurisdiction.
Wash.	Incorrigible truant	Shall be committed to state reform school.
Wis.	Incorrigible child	May be committed to school or association of same religious faith as child.

son," "disorderly person," "incorrigible truant," and incorrigible child" are each used twice. Nine other terms are used once each.

Power is given the courts under the law to have such children taken from their homes and confined in institutions for their especial care. These schools are in general of three kinds: state schools, local public schools, and private schools. The local public schools are called parental schools and children's homes. In less severe cases, it is likely that children sent to such local schools are permitted to stay at home. The private schools include those under the control of religious bodies which accept children of their faith on agreement with the court and sometimes with the parent. Massachusetts has provided county training schools for the custody of habitual truants. This state also, as well as Indiana and Rhode Island, makes provision for paroling such children to their parents, an attendance officer, or a probation officer.

The provisions for local correctional schools and for paroling are recognitions of the desirability of keeping a child in the home, if possible, at the same time that the correctional sentence of the court is operative. They are recognitions, too, of the fact that offenses of this kind vary in degree of gravity and that there should be a range of punishments from the mild to the very severe. Such a range would be included in being paroled to the parent and in being sentenced for several years to a state school. As a mitigation of sentences, the laws of California and Massachusetts permit the court to parole children after a part of the original court sentence has been served, provided the city superintendent, board of education, or county superintendent recommend such parole. Another method of mitigation is provided in the Colorado law, in accordance with which the court may suspend commitment during the time the child regularly attends school and conducts itself properly.

The sections of the Colorado law defining a juvenile disorderly person and the manner of disposition illustrate well the provisions for court action in dealing with this class of offenders. A juvenile disorderly person is defined as follows:

> Every child within the provisions of this act who does not attend school, as provided in section one of this act, or who is in attendance at any public, private, or parochial school, and is vicious, incorrigible, or im-

moral in conduct, or who is an habitual truant from school, or who habitually wanders about the streets and public places during school hours without any lawful occupation or employment, or who habitually wanders about the streets in the night time, having no employment or lawful occupation, shall be deemed a juvenile disorderly person, and be subject to the provisions of this act.[18]

The section on the disposition of such cases by the court is as follows:

Whenever a child shall be a juvenile disorderly person within the meaning of this act, the truant officer, or any school teacher, or other reputable person, may make complaint in the county court in which such child resides. The county court shall hear and determine such complaint, and if it is determined that such child is a juvenile disorderly person within the meaning of this act, he or she shall be committed to a children's home, if eligible, or to the boys' industrial school or to the girls' industrial school, or to some other training school, taking into account the years of the child with reference to the institution selected. Any child committed to a children's home, on its being shown to the judge of said court that it is incorrigible and vicious, may be transferred to the industrial school or other proper institution. No child committed to any reformatory shall be detained beyond its majority, and may be discharged sooner or paroled by the trustees or board of control under rules and restrictions applicable to other inmates. Any order of commitment may be suspended by the judge of the county court during such time as the child may regularly attend school and properly conduct itself. The expense of the transportation of the child to the juvenile reformatory, and of the costs of the case in which the order of commitment is made, shall be paid by the county from which the child is committed.[19]

FUNCTIONS INVOLVING NO PENALTIES

In the attendance laws, a considerable number of court functions are defined which do not require the imposition of a penalty by the court. Table 25 shows these functions and the state or states in which each applies. Functions 1 to 7 inclusive are concerned with the general condition of indigence. Seven different states make specific provisions for having cases of economic need or distress heard by the courts. The issue may be raised as to whether these are not mostly administrative functions that should be performed by the schools or other administrative officers rather than judicial functions to be assigned to the courts. The point may be clarified by noticing the rela-

[18] Colorado School Laws, 1917, p. 42.
[19] *Ibid.*, p. 44.

tion of Functions 3 to 6. In 3, the court hears the case and reports to the school board what the needs are. In 6, the school board evidently hears the case and reports to the court what the needs are. Such matters could be taken care of at once by the school authorities, under proper legislation, without burdening the courts with them. These are not usually matters of controversy involving the necessity of adjudication. Where conflicts did arise, the law could provide for a recourse to the courts for settlement.

TABLE 25

Court Functions and States Involving No Penalties in Attendance Laws

Function	States
1. Determine if parents are unable to provide books and clothes	Ala., Ariz. Ark. (counties having no superintendent of schools)
2. Exempt children whose services are needed to support widowed mothers	N. C.
3. Hear cases where parent makes an affidavit that he needs the labor of the child for support, and transmit findings to the school boards concerned	
4. Make allowances provided by law for the relief of widowed mothers, and use discretion as to continuing or modifying allowance before the child becomes fourteen	Okla.
5. Investigate cases of children neglected and dependent and not attending school, on the report of the county superintendent, truant officer, or probate officer, and appoint boys to the county home	Okla.
6. Investigate and provide relief in cases of children reported by boards of education as lacking clothing or food	Tenn.
7. Try cases of indigent parents and acquit them and adjudge the children dependent	Va.
8. Appoint probation officers	Ariz., Ida.
9. On recommendation of county superintendent fix the occupation of the county school attendance officer and the expenses of such officer as approved by the county superintendent	Mo.
10. Approve appointment of probation officer as county attendance officer	Ohio

TABLE 25 (*Continued*)

COURT FUNCTIONS AND STATES INVOLVING NO PENALTIES IN ATTENDANCE LAWS

FUNCTION	STATES
11. On refusal of parent give orders for attendance officer to take forcible corporal custody of a child	Tex.
12. Issue warrants for the arrest of persons charged with violating the compulsory attendance law, notifying them of the charge, and time and place of hearing	Ark., Conn., Ill., Ky., Mass., Mich., Minn., N. J., Ore., S. Dak., Wis.
13. Instruct grand juries in the various counties at each term of court with reference to the provisions of the compulsory attendance act, who shall investigate all cases of nonattendance reported to them or brought to their attention and return indictments in accordance with the evidence and the facts	Ark., N. Mex.
14. Require properly attested birth certificates	Ark.
15. On recommendation of city superintendent, board of education, or county superintendent, may parole a child which the court has committed...	Calif., Mass.
16. Hear applications for exemption, on appeal from city or county superintendent	Colo., Ida.
17. Exempt children from attendance for sufficient reason	Iowa
18. Hear appeals from refusal of superintendent of schools to excuse children from attendance at part-time schools	Ohio
19. Hear cases against school committees, where children are refused admittance to public school ..	Mass.
20. Receive reports about county training schools for truants from departments of education and public welfare	Mass.
21. Make orders relative to payment by parents of the cost of a child's support while at a county training school	Mass.
22. In cases of home instruction, determine if it is equivalent to instruction in the local day school	Mo.
23. Decide case of mental or physical incapacity on appeal from attendance officer	Mo.
24. County judge to serve on a board for the general supervision of a county home for dependent and neglected white boys	Okla.
25. Receive custody of children whose parents have sufficient income to educate and maintain them, but who refuse or neglect to send them to school	Okla.

The Minnesota law may be cited as an example of legislation whereby indigence as it affects children of school age is regarded as a matter to be treated administratively by the school authorities without requiring judicial action by the court. The provisions of that law for the relief of indigent children of school age are as follows:

Every Board of Education or school board of any school district shall investigate or cause to be investigated, by a truant officer or other authorized officer, all cases reported to it or coming to its knowledge of any child within its jurisdiction required by law to attend school that it is claimed to be unable to do so by reason of the fact that the services of such child are required for the support of himself or herself, or to assist in the support or care of others legally entitled to his or her services, such person or persons being unable to support or care for themselves, and when such Board of Education, or school board shall report to the county auditor of the county in which the school district is situated the facts as ascertained by them and that such relief is necessary, and thereupon the county board may after investigation furnish such relief as will enable the child to attend school during the entire school year, such relief to be furnished by such county board from the poor fund of such county, and the Board of Education or school board of the school district shall furnish for the use of such child the necessary textbooks free of charge.[20]

Indiana, Michigan, and Oklahoma may be cited as other states which provide that defined cases of indigence shall be disposed of as a direct matter of administration through the school officials.

Other functions on this chart indicate a disposition by some states to burden the courts with activities that should be taken care of, and are taken care of, administratively by the schools. Such is Function 13 where so simple a matter as charging a violation of the attendance law is handled by an indictment of the offender by the grand jury rather than by the action of school officials making a direct charge in court. Functions 22 and 23 are also of the kind that should be disposed of directly by the school officials.

It seems evident from the data given in Table 25 that courts have some functions assigned to them by legislation which are not essentially judicial and which should be and are handled in some states as functions of administration by school officials.

[20] Minnesota School Laws, 1923, p. 86.

Summary

1. The courts most frequently designated in attendance laws as having jurisdiction in cases involving these laws are local courts. As such courts are sensitive to local influences, the enforcement of attendance laws is probably affected accordingly.

2. Penalties for violating the attendance laws are confined mostly to three classes of people; namely, parents, employers, and children beyond the control of parents. These penalties require conviction in court on a charge, and the imposition of the penalty by the court.

3. The courts impose penalties for adults of money fines and imprisonments and for children, confinement in correctional institutions.

4. In general, a wide discretion for the court in fixing the severity of the penalty is provided in the laws. A few laws limit the discretion in such a way as to raise the question whether they do not interfere with proper enforcement.

5. Judged by the penalties in the law, the offenses of employers are more serious than those of parents.

6. With a few exceptions, no clear relationship exists between the fines for an offense and the alternative prison penalties.

7. Few states provide for penalizing school officials for failure to perform the duties imposed by the attendance laws.

8. A few states define offenses involving falsification, deception, and evasion. The sources of information that form the basis for adequate enforcement are not in general well safeguarded.

9. Attendance officers are not properly protected in the laws by definitions of what constitutes interference with their work, and fixing adequate penalties for such interference.

10. Penalties on children beyond the control of parents show provisions for grading the punishment from very mild to very severe. Provisions for local correctional institutions and for paroling are numerous.

11. A considerable number of functions is assigned to the courts in the attendance laws which do not involve the adjudication of controversies or the imposition of penalties. The question may be raised as to whether most of these functions do not

belong in the field of administration rather than in the field of judicial decision.

12. The state laws that specify functions for courts in enforcing school attendance are in general inadequate in the following matters:

A. Locating jurisdiction.
B. Adjusting penalties.
C. Defining the duties of officials and others under the attendance laws and providing for appropriate penalties.
D. Safeguarding information.
E. Relieving courts of administrative functions.

CHAPTER V

COURT CASES AND PRACTICES IN NEW YORK CITY AND PHILADELPHIA

In order to discover what the actual work of courts is in their functions of enforcing school attendance in the cases of parents and children who are violating the law, a study was made of this work in the courts of New York City and Philadelphia. These cities were chosen for intensive study and investigation for two reasons. First, they both have a large number of attendance cases in which the school through the attendance department appeals to the courts. Second, they both have well developed attendance departments which have perfected their practice over a number of years in dealing with attendance cases both outside the court and before the court.

SOURCES

The source of material for this part of the study was threefold. There was, first, attendance at hearings of cases as they were disposed of by the court. More than two hundred such cases at six different court sessions were attended in New York City. About thirty-five cases at one session of the court were heard in Philadelphia. A second source of material was the records kept of attendance cases by the courts and by the school attendance departments. A third source was the transcripts of the court stenographers' notes of cases. Fifty-eight such transcripts were secured from the court of the Borough of Manhattan in New York; fifty-five from the Borough of Brooklyn, and forty-eight from the City of Philadelphia. The hearing of the cases had led to the conclusion that the courts perform more functions than the formal record discloses, and that only a careful study of the stenographic transcripts would reveal these functions. This conclusion was amply verified by an intensive analysis of these transcripts. The results of this analysis follow in this chapter.

NUMBER OF CASES HEARD AT COURT SESSIONS

An obvious element in the court practices of both New York City and Philadelphia is the saving of time by disposing of as large a number of cases as possible at each session of the court. With hundreds of cases to be heard each year, to hear each case without loss of time is a matter of economy both for the state and for the parents and children concerned. Where so many cases must be heard and disposed of, it is clear that each one cannot be tried before a jury with contending lawyers and witnesses on each side to prolong the controversy. Such a lengthy procedure would make the expense in time and money so great that the state could not afford to prosecute so many cases, and appeal to the courts by the schools, representing the state, would be precluded. Hence, most of the cases are tried directly by the judge, usually without lawyers, and with as little formality as possible. The charge against a parent or child is presented in a brief and regular form by the school attendance department. Following the charge, the judge questions the defendant and hears any explanation he may offer. The court procedure is such as to expedite the hearing of each person's case and to save as much time for the person as is consistent with bringing before the court all the facts relevant to the case. Several judges mentioned to the writer that the defendants were away from their work or business and that they regarded this loss of time as a part of the penalty in the case.

In the New York City courts, the defendant is required to enter a plea of guilty or not guilty to the charge. If he pleads guilty, the hearing is usually very brief, lasting only a few minutes. If he pleads not guilty, he is given a trial. This means that the complainant in the attendance department gives sworn testimony in support of the charge, and that the defendant's testimony also is taken on oath. Such a trial requires more time than a hearing where the plea of guilty is made. In the Philadelphia court, no plea is required of the defendant. The charge is presented by a representative of the attendance department, and the judge proceeds at once to question the defendant and to hear his explanations.

From the court records of New York City, the cases heard during seventy-six court sessions under five different judges were compiled. Table 26 shows the number of cases for each judge, the number of hearings or sessions, and the average number of cases per session. The average number of cases ranges from thirty-two to fifty. Judge A, who heard the average of thirty-two cases, sits in a court which meets twice a week and is in session from about 2 to 5 P. M. The four other judges had their sessions in a court that meets once a week at 10 A. M. The sessions of this court are usually over by 1 P. M. If an unusual number of cases appear, an afternoon session beginning at 2 o'clock is held. At the four complete sessions of this court which the writer attended, cases were heard at the rate of twenty an hour.

TABLE 26

Attendance Cases per Session Heard by Different Judges

Judge	Total Cases	Number of Sessions	Average Per Session
A	422	13	32
B	874	18	48
C	471	11	43
D	763	17	45
E	853	17	50

RECORDS OF CASES ACCORDING TO PLEA

The court records of New York City permit compiling data on the attendance cases according to the pleas of the defendants. The cases can be classified under the headings of plea of guilty, plea of not guilty, and no plea. Table 27 shows a total of 3,383 cases under five different judges classified in this way. More than half of the people who come before these courts plead guilty to the charges brought by the school attendance department. In such cases, the defendant admits the facts stated by the complainant and does not claim to have a lawful excuse for violating the law. More than fifteen per cent of those appearing in court on the charge of violating the attendance law plead not guilty. Such a plea means that the defendant either denies the charges made, or, if admitting the charges as facts, claims to have legal reasons for apparently not complying with the law. Such a plea means a controversy between the school attendance department and the defendant, and the court holds a formal trial to determine the case. Nearly thirty per cent of the cases enter no plea. The person is neither convicted nor acquitted. A later table will show what the elements are in cases where no plea is entered.

TABLE 27

ATTENDANCE CASES ACCORDING TO PLEA HEARD BY DIFFERENT JUDGES

JUDGE	TOTAL CASES	PLEA GUILTY	PER CENT OF TOTAL	PLEA NOT GUILTY	PER CENT OF TOTAL	NO PLEA	PER CENT OF TOTAL
A	422	271	64.22	96	22.75	55	13.03
B	874	508	58.12	120	13.73	246	28.15
C	471	227	48.20	106	22.50	138	29.29
D	763	382	50.06	85	11.14	296	38.79
E	853	483	56.62	122	14.30	248	29.07
Total	3,383	1,871	55.30	529	15.63	983	29.06

CONVICTIONS IN CASES OF PLEAS OF NOT GUILTY

It is desirable to know what the court decisions are in the controverted cases where the defendant pleads not guilty. In these cases, a contest is on between the attendance department of the schools and the defendant, usually a parent. The attendance department submits what it claims are facts to prove a violation of the compulsory education law. The defendant submits what he claims are facts to prove that he has not violated the law. The court, after hearing both sets of facts and getting all the information it thinks relevant bearing on the case, must render a decision based on the facts and on the law. Table 28 shows that in slightly more than ninety per cent of the five hundred twenty-nine cases where the plea of not guilty was made by the defendant, the court rendered a verdict of guilty. In other words,

TABLE 28

CONVICTIONS IN ATTENDANCE CASES WHERE PLEA IS NOT GUILTY

JUDGE	PLEADED NOT GUILTY	CONVICTED	ACQUITTED	PER CENT CONVICTED
A	96	81	15	84.37
B	120	113	7	94.16
C	106	96	10	90.00
D	85	68	17	80.00
E	122	119	3	97.54
Total	529	477	52	90.2

slightly less than ten per cent of those who thought they had a valid reason for violating the law were able to prove their case to the satisfaction of the court. This record of convictions may be a measure of the efficiency of the school attendance department. It may also be a measure of the disposition of the court to enforce the attendance law.

NO PLEA CASES

It was shown in Table 27 that twenty-nine per cent of the cases made no plea—neither guilty nor not guilty. The records of the court showing the action of the court in these cases disclose why no plea was made. The papers of four hundred forty-five cases were examined, and in this number one hundred sixty-four were cases in which no plea was made. Table 29 shows the characterization of these cases according to the decision made by the court.

TABLE 29

CHARACTERIZATION OF ATTENDANCE WHERE NO PLEA IS ENTERED

ITEM	NUMBER OF CASES	PER CENT OF TOTAL
1. Child apparently beyond control, defendant diligent	107	65.24
2. Child apparently beyond control	3	1.83
3. Age cases	38	23.17
4. Dismissed on request of complainant	13	7.93
5. Dismissed on illness certificate	3	1.83
Total	164	

Most of them are cases in which the child is beyond the parent's control. When this fact is once established in court, the attendance department may proceed against the child in court. The difference between Item 1 and Item 2 in Table 29 is that in Item 1 the defendant is adjudged diligent; in Item 2 such a judgment is not made. Item 3 includes the age cases. Where a birth certificate or other legal evidence is lacking concerning the age of a child, the court on other evidence, usually a physician's certificate or testimony, adjudges the child to be a certain age. Item 4 means that the complainant, the attendance department, after filing a case, finds sufficient reason for having it dismissed.

PENALTIES OF COURTS

The cases subject to penalty by the court are those where the plea is guilty or where the plea is not guilty, but the defendant is found guilty. In disposing of such cases, the courts have a number of alternatives. They may impose a sentence of fine or jail. Such a sentence gives the defendant a choice of paying the fine specified, or of going to prison for the time specified. The courts may suspend sentence, which means that while the defendant is adjudged guilty no actual punishment is imposed, on the condition that in the future the defendant will comply with the law. The penalty may be a fine only, or a jail sentence only. It may consist of placing the defendant on probation for a specified time with conditions as to reporting regularly. The last three kinds of disposition are very rare. The penalty of confinement in a parental school is imposed on children over fifteen who have been adjudged beyond control of parents. In New York City, children under fifteen are tried in the Children's Court.

Table 30 shows the dispositions in 2,348 cases subject to penalty in the New York City municipal term courts. The cases are classified so as to indicate how different judges dispose of their hearings. Part I of Table 30 gives the number disposed of under each kind of penalty. Part II shows the per cent each kind of disposition is of the total. It indicates to some extent how judges differ in disposing of cases under the same law, in the same state and community. Judge A imposed a fine or jail sentence in eighty-five per cent of his cases; Judge B in fifty per cent. Judge A suspended sentence in ten per cent of his cases; Judge B in forty-six per cent of his cases; and Judge D in thirty-nine per cent. The per cents of fine or jail and of suspended sentence for the different judges show wide variations in practice. These per cents are measures of how judicial discretion manifests itself. No measure as to which of these differing ways of disposing of cases subject to penalty are the more effective could be found. If each judge served only one and the same district over a period of time, the number of cases of the same defendant being brought to court a second time or more for the same offense might be a measure of the effectiveness of the court's actions. But in Table 30, Judges A, B, C, D, and E take turns with one another and with other judges in hearing cases in the same court. A case tried as a first offense under one judge is likely to occur as a subsequent offense under other judges.

TABLE 30

PART I

DISPOSITION BY THE COURT IN ATTENDANCE CASES SUBJECT TO PENALTY

Judge	Subject to Penalty	Fine or Jail	Suspended Sentence	Fine Only	Jail Only	Probation	Parental School
A....	352	302	36	0	0	14	0
B....	621	316	287	7	0	0	11
C....	323	238	80	0	3	0	2
D....	450	267	179	1	0	0	3
E....	602	470	114	2	0	0	16
Total	2,348	1,593	696	10	3	14	32

PART II

PER CENT EACH NUMBER IN PART I IS OF TOTAL

Judge	Subject to Penalty	Fine or Jail	Suspended Sentence	Fine Only	Jail Only	Probation	Parental School
A....	352	85.80%	10.22%	0.00%	0.00%	3.97%	0.00%
B....	621	50.88%	46.21%	1.13%	0.00%	0.00%	1.77%
C....	323	73.69%	24.77%	0.00%	0.90%	0.00%	0.60%
D....	450	59.33%	39.78%	0.22%	0.00%	0.00%	0.66%
E....	602	78.07%	18.93%	0.33%	0.00%	0.00%	2.66%
Total	2,348	67.84%	29.64%	0.43%	0.13%	0.6 %	1.35%

As indicated in Table 30, the New York City courts imposed an alternative penalty of fine or jail in more than sixty-seven per cent of all the cases. A total of 1,593 such sentences were pronounced out of the 2,348 cases subject to penalty. Table 31 shows the number sentenced to fine or jail by each judge and the number and per cent choosing jail. The per cents choosing jail range from 1.99 to 23.4. A reason for such a wide range may be found in the relationships of the fines to the alternative jail sentences under the different judges. If a judge imposes a relatively low fine and a relatively high alternative jail sentence, the defendant is likely to pay the fine. If, on the other hand, the judge imposes a relatively high fine and a relatively low alternative jail sentence, the defendant is likely to take the jail sentence.

TABLE 31

NUMBER AND PER CENT OF PERSONS CHOOSING JAIL IN ATTENDANCE CASES WHERE SENTENCES ARE FINE OR JAIL

JUDGE	SENTENCED	CHOOSING JAIL	PER CENT
A	302	6	1.99
B	316	38	12.03
C	238	39	16.39
D	267	16	6.00
E	470	110	23.40
Total	1,593	209	13.12

Table 32 indicates that such an explanation is to some extent reasonable. Judge A imposed an average fine of $2.45 and an average jail sentence of 2.4 days. Here the relationship between fine and jail sentence was such as to lead nearly all defendants to choose the fine. Judge E imposed an average fine of $5.91 and an average jail sentence of 1.77 days. Here the fine is so high and the jail sentence relatively so low that nearly a fourth of the defendants chose to go to jail. Other factors, however, seem to be operative in determining the choice of defendants as indicated by the choices under Judges C and D. Here the average fines and average jail sentences under both judges are nearly the same, but the per cents choosing jail are quite different. In the case of Judge C, more than sixteen per cent choose jail; in the case of Judge D, six per cent.

TABLE 32

RELATIONSHIP OF FINE AND JAIL PENALTIES IN ATTENDANCE CASES

JUDGE	AVERAGE FINE	AVERAGE JAIL SENTENCE
A	$2.45	2.4 days
B	3.00	1.34 days
C	3.36	1.7 days
D	3.25	1.73 days
E	5.91	1.77 days

The actual penalties imposed by five different judges in the New York City municipal term courts in fifteen hundred ninety-three cases are shown in Table 33. The penalties in this table—with the exception of the first three, which are jail sentences only—are all alternative penalties. For example, the tenth penalty is to be read: a fine of three dollars or two days in jail;

and the sixteenth: a fine of five dollars or three days in jail. Judge A has a range of penalties from a fine of one dollar or one day in jail to a fine of ten dollars or ten days in jail. He made

TABLE 33

ACTUAL PENALTIES IN ATTENDANCE CASES BY DIFFERENT JUDGES IN NEW YORK CITY COURTS

Penalty		Number Imposed by Each Judge					Total Number of Cases for Each Penalty
Fine	Jail	A	B	C	D	E	
$ 0	or 2 days			1			1
0	or 3 days			1			1
0	or 5 days			1			1
1	or 1 day	42	65	3	47	21	178
2	or 0 days		3				3
2	or 1 day	1	83	68	67	20	239
2	or 2 days	162	4	4	13		183
3	or 0 days		3				3
3	or 1 day	1	19	29	6	9	64
3	or 2 days	1	59	59	68	2	189
3	or 3 days	58					58
4	or 4 days	8					8
5	or 0 days		1		1	1	3
5	or 1 day	2	41	4	5	258	310
5	or 2 days		24	47	36	24	131
5	or 3 days		8	14	10	3	35
5	or 5 days	23		1	2	29	55
6	or 6 days	2					2
10	or 0 days					1	1
10	or 1 day		2			9	11
10	or 2 days		1	1		60	62
10	or 3 days			2	3	6	11
10	or 5 days		1	3	5	3	12
10	or 10 days	2				3	5
15	or 2 days					1	1
15	or 3 days					6	6
15	or 5 days				2	5	7
20	or 2 days					6	6
20	or 10 days					2	2
25	or 5 days		2		2		4
50	or 30 days					1	1
Total Penalties		302	316	238	267	470	1,593
Number of Different Penalties		11	15	15	14	21	

use of eleven different penalties out of the thirty-one in the table in the three hundred and two cases in which he imposed a penalty. Judge E has a range of penalties from a fine of one dollar or one day in jail to a fine of fifty dollars or thirty days in jail. He used twenty-one different penalties in the four hundred seventy cases in which he imposed a penalty. The one penalty most frequently used by all the judges taken together was a fine of five dollars or one day in jail. It was used three hundred ten times. It is noticeable, however, that two hundred fifty-eight of those penalties were imposed by one judge. In the case of another judge this same penalty was imposed only twice, and of another judge four times, and of another five times.

The three cases of jail sentence only were all imposed by the same judge. An exclusive jail sentence is a rare penalty. There were only three out of fifteen hundred ninety-three. Considering only the fines of Table 33, it is seen that 11.17 per cent are for one dollar; 37.92 per cent are for two dollars or less; 58.17 per cent are for less than five dollars; 33.58 per cent are for five dollars; and 8.1 per cent are ten dollars, or more.

All the penalties of Table 33 were imposed under the following provisions of the New York State law relating to compulsory education:

> A violation of Section 624 (duties of persons in parental relation to children) shall be a misdemeanor, punishable for the first offense by a fine not exceeding five dollars, or five days' imprisonment, and for each subsequent offense by a fine not exceeding fifty dollars, or by imprisonment not exceeding thirty days, or by both such fine and imprisonment.

This law gives a wide range for the discretion of courts in inflicting penalties for a violation of the law. Table 33 shows that thirty-one different kinds of penalties were imposed by the five judges. The law would permit many more. For example, none of the possible fines between six and ten dollars were used; or between ten and fifteen dollars; or between fifteen and twenty dollars; or between twenty and twenty-five; or between twenty-five and fifty.

The experience of these New York courts is that more than a third of the penalties should be two dollars or less. This experience should provide matter for consideration for those legislatures that fix a minimum penalty like five dollars. The New York law fixes no minimum penalty either for the first or for subsequent offenses. The judges may use discretion as to how low the penalty shall be. What the law does is to restrain judges by setting a maximum for first offenses, and another maximum for offenses subsequent to the first.

The practice of the Philadelphia court in imposing penalties is shown in Table 34. This table represents a compilation of data on five hundred cases. In 20.40 per cent of the cases, the defendant paid one dollar and fifteen cents; in nearly sixty per cent of the cases, the defendant paid three dollars and fifty cents; in nearly nine per cent of the cases, the defendant paid five dollars and fifty cents. In one case out of five hundred, or two-tenths of one per cent of the total, the defendant paid eight dollars and fifty cents. In eleven per cent of the cases, the board of education paid one dollar and fifteen cents, which is the lowest actual cost in every case. In these cases, where the cost was paid by the board of education, the case was withdrawn from prosecution by the attendance department when the facts were heard in court. Table 35 shows why these cases were withdrawn, and the number withdrawn for each reason.

TABLE 34

Penalties in Attendance Cases in the Philadelphia Court

Paid by Defendant	Paid by Board of Education	Number of Cases	Per Cent of Total
$1.15	....	102	20.40
3.50	....	298	59.60
5.50	....	44	8.80
8.50	....	1	.20
....	$1.15	55	11.00

In the Pennsylvania law, the maximum cost in attendance cases is fixed at three dollars and fifty cents. The actual cost is one dollar and fifteen cents. The court has discretion in imposing either the maximum or actual cost in any case. The fine in a conviction for the first offense is two dollars, which may be remitted in the discretion of the court. For the second and subsequent offenses, the fine is five dollars, which may be remitted in the discretion of the court. In four hundred of the cases in Table 34, a fine of two dollars was imposed and then remitted. This includes all the cases where the defendants paid one dollar

TABLE 35

ATTENDANCE CASES WITHDRAWN FROM PROSECUTION IN THE PHILADELPHIA COURTS

Cause of Withdrawal	Number
1. Moved and cannot locate	11
2. Attending school	9
3. Poverty	7
4. Child taken to Juvenile Court	7
5. Has employment certificate	6
6. No reason given for withdrawal	5
7. Past sixteen	3
8. Urgent reasons	1
9. Child out of city	1
10. Father out of city	1
11. Child ran away	1
12. Child excused	1

and fifteen cents and three dollars and fifty cents. In one hundred two cases, not only was the fine remitted, but the cost required was the actual and not the maximum. In eighty per cent of these five hundred cases, the only payment required of the defendant was the cost, either maximum or actual.

The Pennsylvania law does not provide for an alternative prison sentence, or for a prison sentence to be imposed instead of a fine in the discretion of the court. It provides that in case the cost and fine required by the court are not paid, the defendant may be sent to prison. In the above five hundred cases, two jail sentences of five days each were served, and the costs were paid by the board of education.

As shown in a previous chapter, some states provide in their attendance laws that the courts shall impose heavier penalties in cases of second and subsequent offenses than the penalty in the first offense. Neither the New York nor the Pennsylvania law has such a provision. The courts in these states are left free to use discretion for fixing the penalty of a second offense except that a higher maximum is set to which the court may go, but there is no requirement for the court to impose a heavier penalty for the second than for the first offense.

The practice of the New York City and Philadelphia courts in imposing penalties in first and second offenses indicates whether they have found the second offense more grave than the first. Table 36 shows the relations of penalties in first and second offenses for forty-three cases in New York City and for fifty cases in Philadelphia. Court records that show which offenses are second offenses and what the penalties for first and second appearances in court were are difficult to secure. To get the forty-three cases from the New York City records, the original papers of the cases filed away in the criminal court building were examined. A total of four hundred forty-five papers were examined to secure forty-three cases of second offenses. In Table 36, it is seen that the penalty for second offenses in New York City is the same as for the first in sixteen per cent of the cases; greater than the first in forty-four per cent of the cases; and less than the first in thirty-nine per cent of the cases. In Philadelphia the penalty for the second offense is the same as the first in seventy per cent of the cases; greater than the first in sixteen per cent of the cases; and less than the first in fourteen per cent of the cases. These figures indicate that legislation which arbitrarily requires a higher penalty for a second than for a first offense is not wise.

TABLE 36

RELATIONS OF PENALTIES IN FIRST AND SECOND OFFENSES IN ATTENDANCE CASES

SECOND PENALTY	NEW YORK	PER CENT OF TOTAL	PHILADELPHIA	PER CENT OF TOTAL
Same as first	7	16.27	35	70.00
Greater than first	19	44.18	8	16.00
Less than first	17	39.53	7	14.00
Total	43		50	

RECURRING OFFENSES

The number of times cases are heard as second or subsequent offenses may be some indication of the effectiveness of court action. If a parent has been convicted of an offense against the attendance law and later reappears one or more times for the same offense, it is an indication that previous actions by the court have not secured conformance to the requirements of the law. A case is a recurring offense where a parent is brought into court more than once because of violations of the law. In such cases, the court often, if not usually, takes into account the fact as to whether the second appearance, or appearances subsequent to the first, is for the same child or not. If the appearance is for the same child, the court is likely to consider its efforts on previous appearances of no avail. If the appearance is for a different child, the defendant is likely to be credited with having remedied the conditions for which he was previously tried. A second appearance on account of a different child is not so serious an offense as a second appearance on account of the same child.

Table 37 shows the distributions of fifteen hundred forty-one recurring offenses for Philadelphia and eighteen hundred sixty-seven for New York City. The number and per cent of cases in each city are given, ranked according to the number of previous appearances in court. In Philadelphia, nearly eighty per cent and in New York City more than eighty-three per cent appear only once. In Philadelphia, more than fifteen per cent and in New York City more than thirteen per cent appear twice, or as second offenders. In Philadelphia, more than three per cent and in New York City less than two per cent appear as third offenders. The fourth and fifth offenders in each case are less than one per cent of the total.

If similar per cents for a large number of cities were available, standards for the effectiveness of court action as shown by the recurring offenses might be set up. In the absence of such standards, the per cents in Table 37 offer only a general indication of effectiveness.

TABLE 37

Recurring Offenses in Attendance Cases

Times in Court	Philadelphia		New York City	
	Number	Per Cent of Total	Number	Per Cent of Total
1	1,232	79.94	1,554	83.23
2	242	15.70	260	13.92
3	50	3.24	37	1.98
4	12	.77	13	.69
5	4	.25	3	.16
6	1	.06	0	0.00
Total	1,541		1,867	

ATTENDANCE AS A MEASURE OF COURT ACTION

The offense for which parents are prosecuted in court under the compulsory education laws is failure to secure the required attendance by their children at school. Before they are brought into court, a record has been made of unlawful absences. If the court has any effect in producing a change in conduct, this effect can be measured by a comparison of attendance before court action with attendance after court action.

The records of attendance of one hundred five pupils in the Philadelphia schools before settlement of their cases in court and after settlement were secured. In choosing the court cases from the records of the attendance department, the following standards of selection were used:

1. A pupil must be of compulsory school age during the entire year.

2. A pupil must be in attendance at a day school during the entire day; no continuation school pupil was selected.

3. A pupil must have been in Philadelphia and subject to the attendance law from the first day of school, September 9, 1925, up to and including the day on which the records of attendance were assembled, which was May 14, 1926.

4. As many pupils as possible were selected from the months of November, December, and January in order to have as long a record as possible on each side of the court action.

The form of keeping the record of attendance of a pupil in the Philadelphia schools is such that the pupil's record before and after any date in the year can be secured accurately in a few moments of time. The number of school sessions for each month of the entire school year is shown on one form. Counting two sessions to a day, the form for the current year shows thirty-two sessions for September, forty-four for October, thirty-eight for November, thirty-four for December, thirty-eight for January, thirty-six for February, forty each for March and April, and up to May 14, twenty in May. The total number of sessions to be accounted for in the case of each pupil was three hundred twenty-two.

In the records of the attendance department, the date of settlement of the case of each pupil was secured. From the pupil's teacher, his record of unlawful absences before the date of settlement and after the date of settlement was obtained. Then with the use of the form for keeping the record of attendance, the total sessions of school before the date of settlement and after the date of settlement were computed. By subtracting from the total number of sessions the number of sessions that the pupil was absent unlawfully, the sessions actually attended before and after settlement were found. By dividing the sessions attended by the total sessions, the per cents of attendance both before and after settlement were secured. These per cents permit the comparison by which the effect of court action is measured.

Table 38 shows the data described for the hundred five pupils. A number is used for a pupil instead of the pupil's name in the first column. Then follow the date of court settlement of the case, the total sessions of schools before settlement, the sessions

TABLE 38

EFFECT OF COURT ACTION ON SCHOOL ATTENDANCE IN PHILADELPHIA

Pupil Number	Date of Settlement	Before Settlement			After Settlement		
		Total Sessions of School	Sessions Absent Unlawfully	Per Cent of Attendance	Total Sessions of School	Sessions Absent Unlawfully	Per Cent of Attendance
1	12/15/25	136	60	55.88	186	0	100.00
2	12/10/25	130	28	78.46	192	18	90.62
3	11/20/25	106	69	34.90	216	25	88.42
4	1/21/26	176	80	54.54	144	17	88.20
5	1/ 5/26	152	72	52.63	170	30	82.35
6	1/26/26	182	64	64.83	140	17	87.85
7	11/20/25	106	53	50.00	216	108	50.00
8	1/26/26	182	157	13.73	140	27	80.71
9	3/11/26	240	112	53.33	82	0	100.00
10	1/21/26	176	57	67.62	146	0	100.00
11	4/ 6/26	266	173	34.96	56	9	84.00
12	1/19/26	172	67	61.00	150	0	100.00
13	1/21/26	176	86	51.13	146	39	73.28
14	11/17/25	98	96	2.00	230	0	100.00
15	12/15/25	136	61	55.15	186	11	94.00
16	12/ 8/25	126	97	23.00	196	0	100.00
17	12/22/25	146	93	36.30	176	6	96.60
18	12/22/25	146	89	39.00	176	13	92.61
19	1/ 5/26	152	150	1.30	170	0	100.00
20	1/ 7/26	156	60	61.54	166	13	92.16
21	12/10/25	130	16	87.70	192	0	100.00
22	1/12/26	162	150	7.40	160	38	76.25
23	12/ 1/25	116	56	51.72	206	24	88.35
24	11/24/25	110	49	55.45	212	0	100.00
25	11/25/25	112	45	59.82	210	0	100.00
26	1/21/26	176	77	56.25	146	0	100.00

TABLE 38 (*Continued*)

Pupil Number	Date of Settlement	Before Settlement			After Settlement		
		Total Sessions of School	Sessions Absent Unlawfully	Per Cent of Attendance	Total Sessions of School	Sessions Absent Unlawfully	Per Cent of Attendance
27	12/22/25	146	70	52.05	176	0	100.00
28	3/25/26	260	190	26.92	62	20	67.74
29	2/18/26	212	96	54.71	110	0	100.00
30	1/21/26	176	88	50.00	146	140	4.11
31	2/23/26	216	216	0.00	106	59	44.34
32	2/ 2/26	174	111	36.09	148	94	36.48
33	3/ 2/26	226	226	0.00	96	92	4.16
34	11/25/25	112	112	0.00	210	0	100.00
35	1/ 5/26	152	100	34.21	170	0	100.00
36	2/ 2/26	174	171	1.75	148	2	98.64
37	12/22/25	146	109	25.34	176	64	63.63
38	2/ 9/26	200	97	51.50	122	16	86.88
39	1/ 5/26	152	120	19.73	170	4	97.64
40	12/22/25	146	146	0.00	176	22	87.50
41	11/20/25	106	67	36.79	216	6	97.22
42	1/12/26	162	162	0.00	160	88	45.00
43	12/ 3/25	120	115	4.16	202	23	88.61
44	11/25/25	112	112	0.00	210	0	100.00
45	1/28/26	186	80	57.00	136	23	83.16
46	12/ 3/25	120	99	17.50	202	41	79.70
47	12/22/25	146	16	89.04	176	6	96.59
48	12/17/25	140	140	0.00	182	6	96.70
49	12/ 8/25	126	126	0.00	196	24	87.75
50	2/ 2/26	174	150	13.79	148	10	93.24
51	1/21/26	176	150	14.77	146	40	72.60
52	1/12/26	162	148	8.64	160	10	93.75
53	2/11/26	204	147	27.94	118	20	83.05
54	11/24/25	110	72	34.54	212	10	95.27
55	1/19/26	172	162	5.81	150	6	96.00
56	1/26/26	182	133	26.92	140	0	100.00
57	2/ 4/26	194	113	41.75	128	38	70.31
58	2/18/26	222	131	40.99	100	40	60.00
59	11/25/25	112	90	19.64	210	32	84.76
60	12/22/25	146	139	4.79	176	28	84.09
61	12/22/25	146	118	19.17	176	62	64.77
62	1/28/26	186	78	58.06	136	24	82.35
63	11/17/25	92	58	36.95	230	10	95.65
64	1/12/26	162	68	58.02	160	22	86.25
65	11/20/25	106	106	0.00	216	83	61.57
66	12/22/25	146	30	79.45	176	22	87.50

TABLE 38 (*Continued*)

Pupil Number	Date of Settlement	Before Settlement: Total Sessions of School	Before Settlement: Sessions Absent Unlawfully	Before Settlement: Per Cent of Attendance	After Settlement: Total Sessions of School	After Settlement: Sessions Absent Unlawfully	After Settlement: Per Cent of Attendance
67	2/ 2/26	174	96	44.89	148	30	79.73
68	11/20/25	106	54	49.05	216	33	84.72
69	11/20/25	106	52	50.94	216	16	92.59
70	3/ 4/26	230	136	40.86	92	1	98.91
71	1/26/26	182	74	59.34	140	44	68.57
72	12/15/25	136	110	19.11	196	10	94.84
73	1/26/26	182	61	66.48	140	0	100.00
74	12/ 8/25	126	50	60.31	196	10	94.89
75	2/11/26	204	129	36.76	118	0	100.00
76	11/24/25	110	88	20.00	212	67	69.39
77	12/22/25	146	122	16.43	176	0	100.00
78	12/17/25	140	96	31.42	182	0	100.00
79	12/ 3/25	120	22	81.66	202	0	100.00
80	2/ 2/26	174	174	0.00	148	0	100.00
81	11/17/25	92	92	0.00	230	132	42.60
82	12/ 1/25	116	111	4.31	206	50	75.72
83	1/ 5/26	152	132	13.15	170	51	70.00
84	3/25/26	260	99	61.92	62	14	77.42
85	12/ 1/25	116	116	0.00	206	23	88.83
86	1/26/26	182	95	49.75	140	12	91.42
87	1/21/26	176	57	67.61	146	8	94.52
88	2/ 2/26	174	174	0.00	148	0	100.00
89	11/24/25	110	102	7.27	212	0	100.00
90	12/17/25	140	47	66.42	182	3	98.35
91	1/12/26	162	162	0.00	160	12	92.50
92	11/20/25	106	42	60.37	216	0	100.00
93	12/15/25	136	95	30.14	186	4	97.84
94	12/22/25	146	98	32.87	176	42	76.13
95	12/ 3/25	120	74	38.33	202	108	46.53
96	12/ 3/25	120	60	50.00	202	42	79.20
97	1/19/26	172	64	62.78	150	12	92.00
98	1/26/26	182	122	32.96	140	0	100.00
99	1/19/26	172	63	63.37	150	23	84.66
100	1/26/26	182	73	59.88	140	50	64.28
101	11/19/25	104	60	42.30	218	2	99.08
102	1/26/26	182	38	79.12	140	4	97.14
103	1/19/26	172	19	88.95	150	12	92.00
104	3/23/26	256	126	50.78	66	5	92.42
105	12/ 3/25	120	110	8.33	202	0	100.00

absent unlawfully, and the per cent of attendance, the total sessions after settlement, the sessions absent unlawfully, and the per cent of attendance.

A comparison of the per cents for each pupil before settlement and after settlement shows that there was a loss in per cent of attendance after court action only in the case of pupil 30; there was neither gain nor loss in case of pupil 7; there was only slight gain in cases of pupils 32, 33, 95, and 100. In the case of all the ninety-nine other pupils, large gains in per cents of attendance are shown. Very noticeable is the fact that twenty-eight of these pupils whose parents had to be brought to court because of these pupils' poor attendance before court action made a record of attendance of one hundred per cent after the experience in court.

In Table 39 the per cents of attendance are arranged in step intervals of five per cent from zero to one hundred per cent. The number of pupils whose attendance was within each step interval

TABLE 39

PER CENTS OF SCHOOL ATTENDANCE BEFORE AND AFTER COURT SETTLEMENT IN PHILADELPHIA

Per Cent of Attendance	Number of Cases Before Settlement	Number of Cases After Settlement
0– 4.99	20	2
5– 9.99	5	0
10– 14.99	4	0
15– 19.99	6	0
20– 24.99	2	0
25– 29.99	4	0
30– 34.99	8	0
35– 39.99	7	1
40– 44.99	5	2
45– 49.99	2	2
50– 54.99	12	1
55– 59.99	11	0
60– 64.99	8	5
65– 69.99	4	3
70– 74.99	0	4
75– 79.99	3	7
80– 84.99	1	10
85– 89.99	3	11
90– 94.99		15
95–100.00		42

before and after court settlement is given. More than half the pupils had an attendance of less than forty-five per cent before court action. More than half had an attendance of over ninety per cent after court settlement. The median per cent of attendance before settlement was 37.50; the median per cent of attendance after settlement was 91.50.

Tables 38 and 39 show the measurable effects of court action on the attendance at school of pupils, whose parents have been brought into court. It must be assumed that the work of courts affects attendance on the part of some children whose parents are not brought to court. No tangible measure of this influence of the courts is available.

COURT WARRANTS AND SUMMONS

The power of the court is used to secure the attendance at court of persons charged with violating the attendance law. In both Philadelphia and New York City, the courts use the same processes to secure this attendance. These processes are summons and warrants. The court summons is the first process used. It is a notice to the person receiving it that he has been charged with violating the compulsory education law, and summoning or commanding him to appear at a specified place and at a specified time to answer to the charge. In Philadelphia, the summons is sent through the mail. In New York City, it is delivered in person by the attendance officer. The Philadelphia summons specifies no penalty for failure to appear. The New York City summons in the Borough of Manhattan specifies that, upon failure to appear at the time and place mentioned, the defendant is liable to a fine of not exceeding fifty dollars or to imprisonment of not exceeding ten days, or both. In the Borough of Brooklyn, the penalty to which the defendant is liable for failure to answer the summons is a fine of not exceeding twenty-five dollars.

The summons is a process used in the interest of economy and convenience both for the court and for the defendant. If a person who receives a summons does not appear at the place and time specified, the second process, a warrant, is issued by the court. Under this process, the defendant is taken into custody, that is, arrested at once, is brought to the police station, and, if court is in session, is brought from the station to the court for a hearing. If the court is not in session, the defendant has to furnish bail or stay in the prison attached to the police station until court is in session. It is evident, therefore, that the defendant's interests are being served by the use of the summons as a process to get him to court.

Not all persons on whom the court serves a summons keep the appointment which they are directed to keep. Some ignore the summons, and the court must issue a warrant for their arrest by a police officer or constable. The records of one thousand thirty-five defendants in Philadelphia and of eight hundred forty-two in New York City were compiled with reference to the kind of process on which each was brought to court. Table 40 shows that in Philadelphia more than eighty-three per cent responded to the summons and slightly more than sixteen per cent required the issuance of a warrant by the court. In New York City, more than eighty-six per cent responded to the summons and slightly more than thirteen per cent required a warrant. It may be conjectured that the higher per cent responding to summons in New York City may be due to the penalty specified in the summons. But there is no proof that this is a factor in making the difference. There is no record of a defendant's having had the penalty mentioned imposed. What difference, if any, the failure to appear on summons makes in a defendant's hearing on the charge of violating the attendance law also cannot be discovered. The transcripts of cases show that the court usually questions the defendant who has failed to appear on summons as to why he did not appear. The testimony of attendance officers sometimes throws light on the disposition of a defendant who ignores the summons. If the attendance officer testifies, as some do, that the defendant swore at him when the summons was served, or said he would not attend court, or tore the summons up, or threw it on the floor, or

TABLE 40

DEFENDANTS APPEARING ON COURT WARRANT AND SUMMONS

	Philadelphia		New York City	
	Number	Per Cent of Total	Number	Per Cent of Total
Warrant	172	16.62	113	13.41
Summons	863	83.38	729	86.59
Total	1,035	100.00	842	100.00

refused to receive it, the court has in this conduct some evidence of the disposition of the defendant toward coöperating in fulfilling the requirements of the law.

FACTORS DETERMINING COURT JUDGMENTS

The basic charge on which persons are brought into court for a violation of the attendance law consists of a certified record of days absent from school. Attendance laws are enacted to insure the presence of children of school age in school. Absence from school is the basic offense on account of which the law and the assistance of the courts are invoked by the school authorities. Absence may be, however, only a symptom of other conditions, which the court in its investigations of cases finds and regards as more deserving of penalty than absence itself. If absence alone were in most cases the chief consideration before the court, it would seem that there might be some discoverable relation between the amount of absence as measured in days and the size of the penalty by the court as measured in dollars of fine.

The transcripts of court cases of New York City and of Philadelphia were studied for some evidence of a relationship between amount of absence and size of fine. Since different judges vary widely in the ranges of fines imposed, as has been shown, the days of absence and the penalties imposed by one judge could not be compared with the days of absence and the penalties imposed by other judges. In other words, the variable factor of the standards of judgment of different judges is eliminated by comparing with each other the cases of several judges as to amount of absence and corresponding penalty.

Cases suitable for comparison were found in the transcripts of hearings by three judges. One judge was from the court in the Borough of Brooklyn, one from the court in the Borough of Manhattan, and one from Philadelphia. Table 41 shows the days absent and the corresponding penalty by Judge A in Brooklyn, similar data for Judge D in Manhattan, and data for the court in Philadelphia. Relatively few cases in the transcripts could be used for the purposes of this comparison for the reason that only those cases could be used in which the record of days absent and of penalty imposed was expressed and in which the pupil concerned was attending a full-time day school. Many cases were continuation school cases, or cases that were dismissed after the hearing, or cases in which the number of days absent was not clearly stated. Moreover, the transcripts from New York City included cases from a number of different judges; so that sufficient cases from one judge for the purposes of comparison were not easily found.

TABLE 41

RELATION OF DAYS ABSENT TO PENALTY IN ATTENDANCE CASES

Judge A Brooklyn		Judge D Manhattan		Philadelphia	
Days Absent	Penalty	Days Absent	Penalty	Days Absent	Penalty
29	Probation 1 year	19½	Suspended sentence	129½	$1.15
23	Probation 2 years	27	Suspended sentence	94½	1.15
31	Probation	20	5– 2	69	1.15
23	Suspended sentence	5	15– 5	25	3.50
20	2– 0 *	12	25– 5	48½	3.50
59	3– 3			53	3.50
14	5– 0			15	5.50
6	10–10			64	5.50
10	10–10				
75	10–10				

* Penalties are to be read: $2 fine, no jail sentence, $3 fine or 3 days in jail, etc.

A comparison of the cases of Judge A shows that the size of the penalty bears no relation to the amount of absence. The heaviest penalty, 10-10, is given to the smallest number of days' absence, six days, as well as to the largest number of days' absence, seventy-five. The penalties of suspended sentence and probation are given to absences amounting to twenty-three days, twenty-nine days and thirty-one days respectively. One absence of fifty-nine days gets a penalty of 3-3; an absence of fourteen days gets a penalty of 5-0; and an absence of ten days 10-10. If this judge is consistent in the application of his standards of judgment, there must be other factors than number of days absent determining his penalties. The same thing is observed in the cases of Judge D. The lightest penalty, suspended sentence, which is in fact no penalty at all, is applied to the largest amount of absence. The heaviest penalties are given to the fewest days of absence. In the Philadelphia court the same relation appears; the lightest penalties may be given to the largest number of days of absence. The conclusion to be drawn from these figures is that there must be other factors than amount of absence that determine the judgment of the court.

The transcripts of the cases throw light on what these factors are. Under Judge A, a defendant was put on probation one year when the charge was that his boy had been out of school twenty-nine days and that the defendant had had four previous convictions against him. With two exceptions, this is the largest amount of absence in the cases under this judge. The charges look very serious. Yet the sentence of the court is the lightest possible. The transcript shows that the defendant was a chauffeur, had a large family, and had no children working; that he promised the attendance officer to keep a close watch on his boy. He told the court that he had tried his best to keep the boy in school, and explained that each night he asked him if he had been in school. He explained, too, that the boy had been sick once for a week, that on another occasion he had lost a day by getting up too late, that another time he did not go to school because he had no shoes, and that part of the time the boy's mother signed his probation card. The court evidently was convinced that the defendant was coöperating, that his economic condition was difficult, and that he in good faith had tried his best.

Under this same Judge A, another defendant with six days of absence on the part of his son was given a penalty of ten dollars fine or ten days in jail. This is the fewest days of absence and the heaviest penalty in Table 41 for Judge A. The transcript shows that the defendant had done nothing to keep the boy in school and took the attitude that there was nothing he could do. The attendance officer testified: "I called on the father and stated to him that the boy was absent from school. The father said he sent him to school. I asked him why he didn't look at the boy's probation card, and he shrugged his shoulders." The court asked the defendant if the attendance officer spoke to him. He answered: "Yes, he did speak to me. What can I do?" The reply of the court was: "Take him to school yourself. That is what you were told to do." The defendant admitted that he had been convicted in this court on a similar charge once before. The sentence of the court was as follows: "I am going to fine you ten dollars or ten days in the city prison as a second offender

I am going to try to make you do what the law intends that you should do."

The court was evidently convinced that the defendant was not coöperating; that he did not try to do what the attendance officer asked him to do; and possibly that he was inclined to be defiant. The fact that he was a second offender seemed to weigh heavily against him.

In one case under Judge A, the absence was twenty-three days, but the mild penalty of suspended sentence was imposed. The defendant in this case was a widow. She testified as follows: "I don't work. I am a sick woman. I have three children. They bring in $13.50 a week. A charity organization pays the rent." The boy in the case said he was sick. Sometimes he had a sore throat, and sometimes he had a headache. The court, however, warned him saying: "Young man, you better look out. You are on the road to the truant school." To the mother, the court said: "If you want to keep that boy at home, see that he goes to school. Bring him there at least once. If you don't, we will send him to the truant school." The boy said that he would go to school thereafter, and the court suspended sentence.

In this case the facts that the defendant was a widow with slender support, that the boy showed a disposition to conform, and that this was a first offense were stronger factors than the twenty-three days of absence.

Judge A imposed a sentence of a fine of ten dollars or ten days in jail in the case of a record of ten days' absence. Relatively this is a heavy penalty for that amount of absence. Some of the other factors that determine this sentence appear from a reading of the transcript of the case. This was a third offense. The defendant said: "I don't know what to do with the boy. He promises to go to school and he don't go." The court: "I told you what to do before—take him to school once and put him in the classroom." The defendant said: "I brought him to the school two weeks ago. I don't know what happened to him." The court: "It is up to you to plead guilty or not guilty to this charge." The defendant: "I am guilty." Attendance supervisor: "The defendant does not coöperate with the officer." Attendance officer: "He refused to sign a consent to place him in the truant school, although he admits he has no control over the boy." Here the court pronounced the above sentence.

In this case the facts that it was a third offense, that the defendant admitted he did not know what to do with the boy, that he took the boy to school but did not know what happened to him, that he did not coöperate with the officer, and that he refused to sign a consent to place the boy in the truant school at the same time that he admitted he could not control him—these were the factors more than the boy's record of absence that called forth a heavy sentence from the court.

Under Judge D, the largest number of days of absence in the five cases cited in Table 41 is twenty-seven. Yet suspended sentence, the mildest sentence this judge gave, was pronounced. The facts in the case show that the defendant was a widow with eight children. The defendant stated that she had kept the child at home, first, because the child had not been feeling very well, and second, because the school was too far away from home and the child was afraid to walk through the park.

The court: "What is the matter with walking a couple of blocks to school? Where was the nearest school to where you lived in Italy, a couple of towns away?"

The defendant: "The girl has to go through Morningside Park, and there are a lot of crooks around there and the child is afraid."

A friend of defendant: "They have a school in 129th Street that is nearer this woman's home. To go to the new school the children have to go through the park. There are a lot of colored people in the block."

The court: "You never had colored people in that block. I lived there for years. Don't tell me that. The child is going to the school she is sent to. How is this woman living? Where does she get any money to live?"

Friend: "She has one son working."

The court (to defendant): "You send that girl to the school she is told to go to; that child has got to go to that school; they have enlarged that school and have plenty of room in it, and haven't room in the other one. I will suspend sentence, but don't you come in again. We will have that child taken away from you if you don't send her to school."

The factors that appear to have affected the court's sentence here are that the defendant was a widow, had eight children to support, had the help of one son only, and had not violated the attendance law before.

In another case Judge D imposed a sentence of a fine of twenty-five dollars or jail for five days in the case of an absence record of twelve days. A reading of the charge and the testimony shows that these facts were before the court as a basis for his judgment: This was the defendant's third offense of this kind. He had been fined five dollars on each of two other occasions, the last time being about three weeks previous to this hearing. He employed his son—the child violating the law in this case—in his business and paid him ten dollars a week. The defendant was a manufacturer of blouses, and his wife worked also. When he was before the court the last time the judge had told him to put the boy back in school. Instead of putting the boy in school, he had kept him out the entire time and put him to work. The defendant had clearly defied the instructions of the court, and was willfully violating the law. Both the defendant and his wife were working, the family was not in want, and the defendant was sacrificing the schooling of his child to the making of money. Relatively the time lost from school was short, but the other factors required a heavy penalty.

A case under Judge D in which the absence record was nineteen and a half days was given a suspended sentence. This was the defendant's first offense; the defendant was a widow; she stated that she sent the child to school and thought he went. The judge talked privately to the boy, and then announced that the boy promised to go to school. On these facts, the court suspended sentence.

In another case Judge D imposed a heavy penalty of fifteen dollars' fine or five days in jail where the absence record was only five days. The facts developed at the hearing were as follows: The defendant was a third offender. The court mentioned the fact that he was a laborer and yet on his previous appearance in court had been fined five dollars, a whole day's pay. The attendance officer testified that he had had a promise from the father on a Saturday that the child would be in school Monday, but that on Monday the boy did not appear. After the father was in court the last time, the boy was out of school two times within the week following. And he was out five times last week. "There is no coöperation of any kind," said the officer.

The court (to defendant): "How much are you getting a day?"

Defendant: "Six dollars a day."

The court: "You haven't done a thing about sending that child to school. This is getting kind of tiresome. You are a third offender. You are fined fifteen dollars or five days in the city prison. The next time you come before me, there will be no fine; imprisonment altogether."

Defendant: "I haven't the money, and don't want to go to jail."

The court: "You are going to pay or go to jail."

In this case, the failure of the parent to coöperate with the attendance officer and his having twice been admonished and fined in court apparently were the factors that caused the judge to impose the heavy sentence.

A case in the Philadelphia court with an absence record of one hundred twenty-nine and a half days received the lowest penalty possible in the sentence to pay the minimum cost of $1.15. The facts brought out at the hearing were that the defendant had a family of twelve children; a relief society had been supplying the children with shoes so they could attend school, and also provided the family with two quarts of milk daily. The father was a workman in a shipyard. This was his first appearance in court for a violation of the attendance law. Before imposing the sentence, the court gave this warning: "You don't take any interest in your family. You are to send these children back to school tomorrow. If you do not comply, I want another warrant issued for next week's hearings."

The large family, their evident poverty, the fact that they were being supported in part by a relief society, and the fact that this was a first offense seem to have been an offset to the large absence record.

In a case with an absence record of fifteen days, this court imposed the relatively heavy fine of five dollars and fifty cents. The testimony at the hearing brought out the fact that the defendant had been fined for the same offense a month before; that the mother and not the defendant took the child to school; that the father did not go to the school to investigate matters when it was reported that the boy ran away from school. On the basis of this testimony the court said: "Why don't you take any interest in the child? That will cost you five dollars and fifty cents or five days in jail."

FACTORS WHERE DEFENDANT WAS GUILTY

All the transcripts of cases where the defendant either pleaded guilty or pleaded not guilty but was found guilty by the court, were analyzed to discover the factors that might affect court judgment in imposing sentence. There were one hundred twenty-nine such cases. In each, the court either imposed an actual penalty or left the way open for imposing one in the future. This analysis was made with the view of discovering what factors or combinations of factors were the probable causes of the different kinds of penalties. It was made, too, with the idea in view that a primary function of the court in hearing and determining cases is to discover and weigh all the factors in each case that are relevant in assisting the court to a just decision.

That the factors that apply to nearly all cases can be isolated began to be apparent after fewer than half of the one hundred twenty-nine cases had been analyzed. Enough factors had been located in the first fifty cases that when a new case was analyzed the factors found in it were nearly all in the list already compiled. As the last cases were analyzed, only occasionally was a factor found that was not already in the list. The following is the list of factors analyzed out of these cases and classified as to kind:

Identification Factors:

1. Defendant failed to send child to school on a specified time and during a specified number of days, or violated the compulsory education law.
2. Defendant had been convicted before on a similar charge.
3. Defendant had never been convicted before on a similar charge.
4. Defendant had been convicted before for the same child.
5. Defendant lived at a specified place of residence.
6. Defendant was the parent of the child in the case or was in parental relation to it.
7. Defendant was a naturalized citizen.
8. Attendance officer at a stated time had spoken to the defendant about his child's absence.
9. Evidence of the child's age was offered and also evidence that he was not a graduate of a high school, and was not in attendance upon instruction at a public, private, or parochial school, or did not have an employment certificate.

10. The school term was nearly over.
11. Defendant was a habitual truant.

Economic Factors:

12. Defendant had a large family.
13. Defendant had a small income.
14. Defendant had no children working.
15. Defendant's rent was paid by a charity organization.
16. Defendant was a widow.
17. Defendant had a comfortable income.
18. Defendant was receiving clothing and food from a relief society.
19. Defendant was poor.
20. Defendant did not need the money from the labor of his child.
21. Defendant needed the child's help as the main support of the family.
22. Defendant was sick and could not support his family by himself.
23. Defendant lived in a condition of extreme poverty.
24. Parents of child were dead; child raised by relatives.
25. The child was the support of the family and was without employment.
26. The mother of the child was not living.
27. The husband had left the family.

Attitude Factors Relating to Child:

28. Defendant promised to coöperate to keep child in school.
29. Defendant took child to school.
30. Defendant examined and signed child's probation card every day.
31. Defendant went to school to inquire about the child's record and attendance.
32. Defendant did nothing to place or keep child in school.
33. Defendant said there was nothing he could do about the child's absence.
34. Defendant was indifferent about examining and signing the child's probation card daily.
35. Defendant admitted not knowing what happened to the child at school.

36. Defendant failed to investigate when it was reported that his child had run away from school.

37. Defendant promised to see that the child went regularly to school.

38. Defendant was indifferent as to the whereabouts of his child.

39. Defendant tried to put the responsibility for keeping his child in school on the attendance officer.

40. Defendant said he did not have time to place his children in school.

41. Defendant said that the boy was working and he, the defendant, needed his help.

42. Defendant offered no reason for boy's absence from school.

43. Defendant failed to bring child to court on request of the attendance officer.

44. Defendant stated that he would like to have the child compelled to go to school, but did not think he was compelled to do it himself.

45. Defendant did not look at and sign the probation card, but a daughter seventeen or eighteen did this.

46. Defendant said to the court: "How was I to know if the boy went to school? I am in business."

47. Defendant told attendance officer he was too busy in his factory to bother about sending his boy to school.

48. Defendant did not see the child's monthly report cards.

49. Defendant tried to evade control of and responsibility for child.

50. Defendant had not talked to child in an attempt to get child to attend school.

51. Defendant was not diligent in trying to find boy who ran away.

52. Defendant or attendance officer submitted evidence that child had been attending school since the case was filed in court.

53. Defendant permitted his child, who was not eligible to an employment certificate, to work.

54. Defendant did not try to control his child.

55. Defendant was unwilling to punish his child to make him go to school, or to discipline him in any way.

56. Defendant admitted to attendance officer that he knew his child was absent.

57. Defendant did not assume responsibility for knowing if his child was in school or not.

58. Defendant sacrificed the schooling of his child in order to have the child make money.

59. Defendant kept the child at home in the house.

60. Child promised to get working papers.

61. Child promised court to go to school.

62. Child will soon be beyond school age.

Attitude Factors Relating to Authority:

63. Defendant was defiant towards the school officers, the law, and the court.

64. Defendant willfully violated the law.

65. Defendant refused to accept a summons from the attendance officer.

66. Defendant assaulted the attendance officer.

67. Defendant assumed that he was more important than the law.

68. Defendant kept the attendance officer going on fool's errands.

69. Defendant threatened to throw the attendance officer out of the house.

70. Defendant said in court that the attendance officer was a liar, and was not telling the truth about his boy.

71. Defendant threw the summons after the attendance officer into the street.

72. Defendant told the court that she would bring her children, and the court could send her and them to jail where they would get free grub.

73. Defendant assaulted a teacher.

74. Defendant refused and failed to get an employment certificate.

75. Defendant unlawfully allowed his child to sell newspapers.

76. Defendant employed a school child who did not have employment certificate.

77. Defendant as employer refused to give a child time off to get an employment certificate.

78. Defendant had been told by the attendance officer that the employer had no objection to the boy going to school, but, nevertheless, did not send the boy.

79. Defendant had been warned not to allow his boy to sell papers after hours, but he said he did not see any harm in the boy making a few pennies.

80. The wife of the defendant refused to tell the attendance officer at what time he could find the defendant at home.

81. The assistant director of attendance refused to exempt the child because the defendant would give no information as to who the child's employer was.

82. Defendant said he was not concerned in the law at all, and nobody could make him send the boy to school if he did not want to go.

83. Defendant refused to sign a consent to place the child in the truant school, while admitting the child was beyond control.

84. Defendant refused to give the attendance officer information about where the child was working.

85. Defendant failed to do what the court or attendance officer suggested to secure attendance.

86. Defendant refused to coöperate with the school or attendance officer.

87. Defendant failed to appear at a hearing called at the attendance department of the board of education.

88. Defendant failed to appear at court on summons and the court was compelled to issue a warrant for his arrest.

89. Defendant told the attendance officer he would not send his child to school.

90. Defendant refused to promise that he would put his child in school.

91. Defendant told the attendance officer that he would rather go to jail than send the child to school.

92. Defendant protested inability to get child to attend school, at the same time that the child was earning money.

93. Defendant gave attendance officer fictitious addresses to which he claimed child had gone.

94. Defendant practiced deception in claiming that a child of twelve working in his place of business was working for her older sister, who worked right next to the younger girl, and was being paid by the piece for her work.

95. Defendant testified that his child was not out of school on dates charged by the attendance department, but that he did not see the child in school.

96. Defendant protested that he wanted to obey the summons to attend the court but his wife told him to look for a job and she would attend court.

97. Defendant told attendance officer that the boy would lose his position if he were required to go to school, but the employer when seen made no objection at all to the boy's going to continuation school.

98. Defendant practiced deception in claiming that her husband was drunk and did not care what he did with the children.

99. Defendant misrepresented the age of his child according to the records of the board of health.

100. Defendant practiced deception in claiming he was sick at the same time that the attendance officer always found him at work at his place of business.

101. Defendant failed to produce the employment certificate of the child and claimed it was lost.

102. Defendant failed to produce the birth certificate of the child and claimed it was lost.

103. Defendant claimed the child was sick, but offered no physician's certificate as proof.

104. Defendant claimed he reported lost child to the detective bureau, but the bureau said it had no record that such a child had ever been reported.

105. Defendant claimed that the boy had run away, while the boy's classmates reported he was at home every night, and neighbors reported he was working to buy clothes.

106. Defendant testified that the principal had told him the boy was in school every day, but on investigation, the principal reported the boy had not been in school.

107. Defendant offered money to the attendance officer if he would not prosecute.

108. Defendant changed baptismal record.

109. Defendant was deceived regarding child's attendance.

Health Factors:

110. Defendant presented an unsworn physician's certificate that the child had been ill.

111. Defendant told attendance officer falsely that child was not living at home.

112. Defendant had sickness in his family.

113. Defendant was sick himself.

114. Defendant had a physician's certificate showing illness of the child.

115. Defendant had physician's certificate that he and his wife were under the physician's care.

116. Child did not keep himself clean.

117. An examination by the school physician showed the child physically fit to go to school.

118. The child of the defendant was in a physical condition that required an operation.

119. The child was sick and in the hospital.

Duty Factors:

120. Attendance officer had done his duty by reporting to the defendant that the child could not be found where he said it was.

121. Attendance officer had done his duty by explaining to the defendant the requirements of the law.

122. Attendance officer had done his duty by instructing the defendant as to what to do to secure attendance by his child.

123. Attendance officer had done his duty by getting information on the economic and health conditions of defendant's family.

124. Attendance officer had himself taken the child to school.

125. Attendance supervisor, when asked by the court to do so, gave his opinion as to what the sentence should be.

This isolating of factors in school attendance cases shows that the court faces a considerable variety of conditions in determining such a case. Discovering the relevant factors in a case and giving each its proper weight in arriving at a decision seems to be one of the primary functions of the court in enforcing compulsory education laws. What the court shall pronounce as its judgment, binding alike on defendant and complainant, requires a survey of all the interests involved. The "first object [of the judge] is to render equal justice between the parties to the case. He wishes to settle their rights and give them remedies for their wrongs as shown in the precise facts of the case."[1] "My analysis of the judicial process comes then to this, and little more: logic, and history, and custom and utility and the accepted standards of right conduct, are the forces, which singly or in combination shape the progress of the law. Which of these forces shall domi-

[1] Hicks, F. C. *Materials and Methods of Legal Research*, p. 41.

nate in any case must depend largely upon the comparative importance or value of the social interests that will be thereby promoted or impaired." [2]

FACTORS IN SELECTED CASES

As already shown in this chapter, judges vary in the degree of lenience or severity with which they render their judgments under the provisions of the attendance law. A study, however, of the judgments and of the factors that apparently were the cause of them shows that certain combinations of factors produce mild sentences and certain other combinations produce severe sentences. In the above cases analyzed, fifty-eight were from the court in the Borough of Manhattan. Fifteen of them had relatively light penalties and twelve relatively severe penalties. The two sets of cases, those with light penalties and those with severe penalties, are shown in Tables 42 and 43. For each case, the penalty is given and under the penalty the numbers of the factors in the above analysis that apply to the case. The numbers occur in the order in which the factors came out in the case.

The transcripts of the cases seldom give an indication as to how the judge rated any single factor in importance. But taking all the factors together, it is usually clear why the judge decided as he did. For example, Case 3 in Table 42 shows that the defendant had violated the education law (1); was a poor man (19); was defiant towards the school officers, the law, and the court (63); had told the attendance officer he would not send his child to school (89); refused to accept a summons from the officer (65); was a naturalized citizen (7); submitted evidence that his child had been attending school since the case was filed (52); and promised to see that the child went regularly to school (37). Here the judge had to weigh some damaging things about the man against some other things that were favorable. His defiance seemed to be more of words than of deeds, for while he spoke defiantly to the officer, he sent the child to school and promised in court to continue doing so. Hence the suspended sentence.

In Case 14 the defendant was poor (19); had been warned not to allow his boy to sell papers after hours, but said he did not see any harm in the boy making a few pennies (79); had a small income (13). Here a light penalty of a fine of one dollar was

[2] *Ibid.*, p. 42. Quotation from Cardozo's *Nature of the Judicial Process*, p. 28.

TABLE 42

Factors in Attendance Cases Where Light Penalties Were Imposed

Case No. 1	Case No. 2	Case No. 3	Case No. 4	Case No. 5	Case No. 6	Case No. 7	Case No. 8	Case No. 9	Case No. 10	Case No. 11	Case No. 12	Case No. 13	Case No. 14	Case No. 15
S. S.	$1 Fine	S. S.	S. S.	S. S.	S. S.	S. S.	S. S.	S. S.	S. S.	S. S.	S. S.	S. S.	$1 Fine	S. S.
28	1	1	21	1	1	1	1	1	1	52	109	1	19	11
61	121	19	16	16	115	16	52	9	16	61	28	16	79	19
52	58	63	81	12	25	52	29	81	52			28	13	52
	53	89		13	10	114	37	121	2			61		
	89	65						78						
	41							21						
	86	7						61						
	12	52												
	14	37												
3	9	8	3	4	4	4	4	7	4	2	2	4	3	3

S.S. = Suspended Sentence.
Numbers refer to the factors listed on pages 164 to 170. For instance in Case No. 1, the factors operating were those enumerated as 28, 61, and 52 in the list.

TABLE 43

Factors in Attendance Cases Where Severe Penalties Were Imposed

Case No. 1	Case No. 2	Case No. 3	Case No. 4	Case No. 5	Case No. 6	Case No. 7	Case No. 8	Case No. 9	Case No. 10	Case No. 11	Case No. 12
$10 Fine	$25 Fine	$10 Fine	3 Days Jail	1 Day Jail	$10 Fine	$25 Fine	$25 Fine	$15 Fine	$15 Fine	$30 Fine	$10 Fine
75	9	1	1	2	1	1	76	1	1	1	76
2	76	2	2	53	2	2	94	2	2	2	101
49	77	110	6	91	32	63		70	28	12	76
		117	111	64		32		6	85	63	102
		66	120			58		63	32	72	
			121			17		40		98	
			4					71			
			58					4			
			93					124			
			63					125			
			32					17			
			12								
			17								
			86								
			91								
			85								
			67								
			125								
			68								
3	3	5	19	4	3	6	2	11	5	6	4

Numbers in columns refer to the factors listed on pages 164 to 170.

imposed no doubt with the view that it was a severe penalty for the defendant and would secure conformance on his part. An additional factor or two would have made this an entirely different case. If this had been a second or third offense, and the man had a good income, and had one or more other children working, the situation before the court would probably have called for a severe judgment.

In Case 6 the defendant had violated the education law (1); had a physician's certificate that he and his wife were under the physician's care (115); the child was the support of the family and was without employment (25); the school term was nearly over (10). These factors taken together called for the mild judgment of suspended sentence.

The severest sentence recorded in Table 43 is given in Case 4. It is the unusual sentence of confinement in prison, and for the relatively long period of three days. This defendant had failed to send his child to school on specified days (1); had been convicted before on a similar charge (2); was the parent of the child in the case (6); told attendance officer falsely that the child was not living at home (111); had been told by the attendance officer that the child could not be found where he said it was (120); had had the requirements of the law explained to him by the attendance officer (121); had been convicted before for the same child (4); permitted the child, who was not eligible to an employment certificate, to work (53); gave the attendance officer fictitious addresses to which he claimed the child had gone (93); was defiant towards authority (63); did nothing to place or keep his child in school (32); had a large family (12); had a comfortable income (17); refused to coöperate with the school or with the attendance officer (86); told the officer he would rather go to jail than send the child to school (91); failed to do what the court or attendance officer suggested to secure attendance (85); assumed that he was more important than the law (67); attendance supervisor's opinion was asked as to what the sentence should be (125); defendant kept the attendance officer going on fool's errands (68). As Table 43 shows, this case is unusual in the number of factors involved and in the fact that scarcely a mitigating factor is in the list.

The case in Table 43 with the next largest number of factors is Case 9. The defendant did not send his child to school on days specified (1); was a second offender (2); said the attendant officer was a liar, and was not telling the truth about his boy (70); was the parent of the child in the case (6); was defiant towards the school in denying the truth of the reported absences of his children (63); said he could not lose a day's work to place his children in school (40); threw the summons after the attendance officer into the street (71); had been convicted before for the same child (4); attendance officer had himself taken his child to school (124); attendance supervisor was asked to give his opinion as to what the sentence should be (125); defendant had a comfortable income (17).

Where such a group of factors form the elements of a case, a severe penalty seems just and proper. The state and its representatives, the school and the school officers, and the children in the case had rights which were being disregarded and actively violated by this defendant. No excuse could be discovered or was discovered by the court either among the economic factors, attitude factors, health factors, or duty factors for this man's conduct. Justice to the best interests of society as represented by the state and by his children as future citizens required that the court dispose of the case in such a manner as to compel this parent to discharge his responsibility to these children, and to conform to the accepted standards of conduct as defined in the enactments of the legislature.

A similar analysis for cases in which the court found the defendant not guilty could be made. Such an analysis is not undertaken because there are too few not-guilty cases in the list of transcripts, and because the above analysis of one hundred twenty-nine cases is regarded as sufficient to illustrate what functions the courts perform in dealing with attendance cases. Moreover, as previously shown in this chapter, the not-guilty cases are a small proportion of the entire number of attendance cases heard.

As a sample of the factors that cause the court to pronounce a defendant not guilty, the following case has been analyzed from the transcripts: Defendant failed to send child to school on specified days; is parent of the child in the case; attendance officer had informed defendant of the requirements of the law; defendant refused to send child to school; defendant was a widow; had three children, sixteen, thirteen, and ten years of age; mother had to make living for family working as a cook; had an income of twenty-two dollars a week; none of the children was working; child told mother she went to school, but did not go; defendant declared not guilty; instructions given to attendance officer to bring child to court to be sent to truant school if she did not go to school voluntarily; child promised to go to school.

An analysis could be made also of factors in the cases heard in the children's court where the defendants are children who have already been adjudged beyond the control of the parent. The transcripts of such cases show that they are relatively simple. The court brings out the identification factors as to the age, residence, and absence record of the child; establishes the health factors, the factors relating to the degree to which the child is beyond control, and the duty factors of school officials. On such factors a usual sentence is one of probation, or committal to a truant school or to a school agreed on between the parent and the court.

COURT FUNCTIONS IN HEARING CASES

From the analysis of the above cases and a study of the other transcripts assembled for this investigation, the following functions of courts in hearing and determining charges of a violation of the compulsory education law are deduced:

A. To discover in each case the factors that affect the guilt or innocence of the defendant. This involves determining the validity of information offered for the court's enlightenment.

B. To decide and announce that the defendant is either guilty or not guilty.

C. If guilty, to determine the degree of guilt in the light of all the factors involved and to impose a suitable penalty. This means giving consideration to the social interests that are to be conserved by the court's decision.

D. To teach parents, employers, and children respect for the law, and the necessity of coöperation with the school.

E. To compel parents to discharge the responsibilities they owe to the children under their control.

F. To declare parents freed from responsibility when children are proven beyond control.

G. To ascertain if attendance officials are doing their duty by properly informing parents, employers, and children regarding the law and their responsibilities under it, and by assembling data pertinent to assisting the court in the formation of its judgment.

SOURCES OF INFORMATION FOR COURTS

It is evident in reading court cases that the soundness of a court judgment is dependent for one thing on the validity of the information presented for the court's consideration. One entire classification of the factors affecting judgments was found to be deception. Some of these deception factors the court might detect unaided during progress of the hearing, but most of them must be disclosed to the court by other parties interested in the case.

The transcripts of one hundred sixty-five cases were searched through for the evidence as to what the sources of information in the cases were. Table 44 gives a summarization of these sources. There it is seen that the parents who are defendants form the largest single group that informs the court. However, if Sources 2 and 3, attendance supervisor and attendance officer, may be regarded as one source and that the attendance department, it is the greatest source, being represented in the one hundred sixty-five cases two hundred twenty-four times.

TABLE 44

SOURCES OF INFORMATION IN COURT CASES INVOLVING THE VIOLATIONS OF ATTENDANCE LAWS

Source	Number
1. Defendant—parent	153
2. Attendance supervisor	141
3. Attendance officer	83
4. Defendant's child	32
5. Physician's certificate or testimony	15
6. Friend of defendant	7
7. Court attendant	5
8. Probation officer	4
9. Defendant's counsel	4
10. Defendant—child beyond control	4
11. Defendant—employer	3
12. Defendant's wife	3
13. Child employed	2
14. Father of defendant—child	2
15. Mother of defendant—child	1
16. Representation of a relief society	1
17. Defendant's brother	1
18. Defendant's sister	1

Considering the fact that the attendance officials represent the school and state, present the charges in every case on which the defendant is tried, are usually able to give the court or to get for the court any information the court thinks necessary to be considered in its judgment, it is evident that they form, or should form, the chief factor of reliability for the court in determining the disposition of cases. The degree of certainty and confidence with which a court functions is therefore largely dependent on the efficiency of the attendance department that makes charges against persons violating the education laws. If an attendance department is organized to function effectively only cases of real merit are brought before the court for adjudication, and they are supported by an array of evidence which not only assists the court to a reasonable disposition but insures an enforcement of the law according to the intent of the legislature.

Summary

1. Court procedure in cases involving compulsory attendance is such as to complete a large number of hearings in a relatively short length of time. Under five different judges, the number of hearings ranged from 32 to 50 to a session.

2. More than half of the people brought before the court in attendance cases plead guilty; more than fifteen per cent plead not guilty. Of those pleading not guilty, more than ninety per cent are found guilty by the court.

3. Judicial discretion manifests itself by wide variations in penalties imposed by different judges hearing cases under the same law.

4. The fixing of minimum penalties such as five dollars by legislation enactment finds no support in the court experiences of New York City and Philadelphia.

5. Fixing a higher penalty by law for a second offense than for a first offense is not approved by the practice of the New York City and Philadelphia courts.

6. Over eighty per cent of cases appear as first offenders only. This may be a measure of the effectiveness of court action or of the work of the attendance department or both.

7. Improvement in the attendance of children indicates that the court has a marked effect on the change of conduct.

8. Over eighty per cent of the defendants in compulsory attendance cases appear in court on a summons.

9. The number of days a child is absent has little, if any, effect on the penalty imposed by the court. Other factors determine the size of the penalty.

10. A primary function of the court is to discover what the other relevant factors in a case are and to use them as the basis for a decision.

11. The attendance department is the chief source of reliable information for courts. The certainty and confidence with which they function is dependent in a large degree on the efficiency of the attendance service.

CHAPTER VI

CONCLUSION

Every state in the Union now has a compulsory education law. Most of these laws were first enacted within the last fifty years. Only eleven states had passed such a law prior to 1875.[1] These laws are undergoing gradual and progressive modifications with the view of requiring attendance at school for a longer period of time each year and for a greater number of years for each child. These modifications include also more and more the means for enforcing the specified periods of attendance.

Among these means are the provisions for appeals to the courts. When the school authorities, representing the state, are unable to secure conformance with the enactments of the legislature regarding attendance on instruction, they have recourse under the law to the courts. It is the duty of the courts to determine to what extent the accused parties are guilty of the offense described and defined by the legislature as a violation of the law compelling attendance at school. Not only is it the duty of the court to determine the degree of guilt but also to impose an appropriate penalty within the law as a punishment. It is evident that in the program for school attendance, the court becomes a decisive factor in the case of that limited group of persons who do not voluntarily seek the privileges of a free public education but who endeavor to evade the requirements of society for attendance on instruction.

This study indicates, however, that before the courts can fulfill adequately the important functions that they are meant to exercise in enforcing attendance laws, some fundamental considerations must be fairly met. In the first place, the school government must have an efficient attendance department. It is the attendance service of the schools which is responsible for bringing cases to the courts. The effectiveness of court action depends very largely on the character of the evidence presented in attend-

[1] Emmons, Frederick E. *City School Attendance Service*, p. 3.

ance cases by the attendance department. The officials who perform the various functions connected with securing proper attendance by all children of school age should be in a position to present fearlessly to the court all relevant facts affecting any case. If local officials are afraid to prefer charges, as may well be the case in small communities, provision should be made by legislation for having such cases brought to court by officials who are not hindered by local friendships. The same may be said in regard to local courts. If the local court in small communities is hesitant about offending neighbors, provision should be made for hearing cases in a court outside the neighborhood. It is important in the interest of adequate enforcement of the attendance law to safeguard both the attendance officials and the court officials so far as local and neighborhood influences are concerned. If legislatures are sincere in passing attendance legislation, they will not permit such legislation to become inoperative through the hindrances that often and almost necessarily attend enforcement by local officials. Judges of local courts in small communities, elected by popular vote, are not likely to enforce a strict attendance law against neighbors. Such are conclusions from the evidence in Chapter II.

The courts have rendered valuable services to the cause of education by the series of recorded judicial decisions in cases affecting compulsory attendance. The courts have been the battle-grounds of hard-fought legal controversies where principles vital to the maintenance of the ideals of universal education have been at stake. The courts have been called upon to consider conflicting interests involving the state, the parent, the child, and the employer. They have had to determine what course of action was binding on these parties in controverted issues. Their decisions have greatly strengthened free, universal, and popular education. In such critical matters as the constitutionality of enactments on compulsory education, the issues involved in the vaccination of school children, the place of private and parochial instruction in the scheme of education, the relation of child labor to compulsory education, and a number of other important items affecting the scope and control of education by the state, the courts have established principles of far-reaching significance. In a body of fundamental arguments, as shown in Chapter III, they have set forth the legal foundations on which such principles rest. So firmly established have some of these principles become, that they are universally accepted and are not questioned by appeal to the courts of any state.

A study of the court functions provided in state attendance laws indicates that legislation along a number of lines is needed before the courts can function adequately in enforcing attendance. Such legislation would safeguard court action in attendance cases against local influences that might tend to nullify the will of the legislature. It would fix a range of penalties that would permit wide discretion to the court in meeting the varying conditions connected with attendance cases. It would define more specifically than is now the case the duties of the various officials who have responsibilities under the compulsory education laws, and would provide for proper penalties for neglect in discharging these responsibilities. It would safeguard the sources of information by defining offenses involving falsification, deception, or evasion and by providing penalties therefor. Finally, it would not assign to the courts functions that belong to the field of school administration.

As supported by the practical experiences of the courts of New York City and Philadelphia, legislation should provide for the speedy hearing of attendance cases so as to save time and expense both for the state and for the defendant. The fixing by law of a higher penalty for the second than for the first offense is not approved by the experience of these cities. Neither is the fixing of a minimum penalty by law approved. Legislation should provide for getting people to appear in court on a summons rather than on a warrant, since this is an effective means of economy in administering the attendance law.

With legislation such as is proposed in the light of this study, school authorities should turn with great confidence to the courts for the assistance they are able to give in the proper and reasonable application of the attendance laws. This study, as shown in Chapter V, gives proof of a remarkable effectiveness of court action in cases involving violations of such a law.

A SELECTED AND ANNOTATED BIBLIOGRAPHY

ADDAMS, G. S., Judge of the Juvenile Court, Cleveland, Ohio. "Recent Progress in Training Delinquent Children." *Report of Commissioner of Education,* 1913. Vol. 1, p. 481.

A description of recent progress in establishing juvenile courts. Tells of their functions and procedures, and increasing scope of work.

BAILEY, WILLIAM B. *Children Before the Courts in Connecticut.* U. S. Department of Labor, Children's Bureau Publication, No. 43. Government Printing Office, Washington, D. C., 1918.

Presents the legislative progress of Connecticut in its dealings with children from 1635 to 1917. Shows gradual change in public opinion concerning the responsibility of child for his unlawful acts. Describes present methods of conducting cases of juvenile delinquents before the courts. Contains a detailed study of juvenile delinquency in certain cities and towns.

BELDEN, EVELINA. *Courts of the United States Hearing Children's Cases.* U. S. Department of Labor, Children's Bureau Publication, No. 65. Government Printing Office, Washington, D. C., 1920.

The study is based on questionnaires sent to judges of juvenile courts, probation officers, and clerks of juvenile courts. The questionnaires were sent to 2,391 courts. Answers were returned by 2,034. The study covers the year 1918. Contains bibliography on reports relating to work of courts hearing children's cases.

BERMEJO, F. V. *The School Attendance Service in American Cities.* George Banta Publishing Co., Menasha, Wis., 1923.

A questionnaire study of attendance service in 371 cities in all parts of the country. An analysis of practice with regard to organization and personnel, the school census, absences and transfers, costs and court cases, and child employment.

BIXLER, EDWARD CLINTON. *An Investigation to Determine the Efficiency with Which the Compulsory Attendance Law is Enforced in Philadelphia.* University of Pennsylvania, Philadelphia, Pa., 1913.

Describes some factors that make attendance laws ineffective and proposes remedies.

BONNER, H. R. "Compulsory Attendance Laws." *American School Board Journal,* December, 1919, p. 39; February, 1920, p. 47.

A study of compulsory attendance laws effective in all the states in 1917-18. Applies fourteen standards to measurement of adequacy of laws.

BONNER, H. R. "The Conviction of Legislators for Failure to Enact Effective Compulsory Attendance Laws." *American School Board Journal,* February, 1923.

Charts significant provisions for compulsory attendance laws in effect January 1, 1923. Discusses the exemption evil and shows how the laws encourage children to play hookey.

BONNER, H. R. "Waste in Education." *American School Board Journal.* July, 1921.

Sets forth the degree of nonattendance for the country as a whole. Shows that it is much greater in some states than in others, and in rural schools than in city schools. Names and explains five leading causes of poor attendance.

BRECKINRIDGE, SOPHONISBA P. and JETER, HELEN R. *A Summary of Juvenile Court Legislation in the United States.* U. S. Department of Labor, Children's Bureau Publication, No. 70. Government Printing Office, Washington, D. C., 1920.

CARROLL, CHARLES. "The Supreme Court and Compulsory Education." *American School Board Journal,* May, 1924, p. 47.

Analyzes the court decisions relative to the Oregon law requiring exclusive attendance in public elementary schools, and the Nebraska law forbidding education in other languages than English in elementary schools both public and private.

CHATFIELD, GEORGE H., Assistant Director, Bureau of Attendance, New York City. "What Provisions Should a Compulsory Education Law Include from the Viewpoint of Aim and the Viewpoint of Enforcement?" *Proceedings of the National Education Association,* 1917, p. 826.

Favors local enforcement rather than state. Law should be specific and plain rather than general.

CHILDREN'S BUREAU, U. S. DEPARTMENT OF LABOR. *List of References on Juvenile Courts and Probation in the United States and a Selected List of Foreign References.* Children's Bureau Publication, No. 124. Washington, D. C., 1923.

CHUTE, CHARLES L. *Probation in Children's Courts.* U. S. Department of Labor, Children's Bureau Publication, No. 80. Government Printing Office, Washington, D. C., 1921.

Discusses the work and meaning of children's courts. Describes at length probation methods and their results.

COBB, B. W. *Inferior Criminal Courts Act of the City of New York.* Macmillan Company, 1925.

Describes the organization of the courts of minor jurisdiction in New York City, their procedures, and their work.

COOPER, RICHARD WATSON and COOPER, HERMANN. *The One-Teacher School in Delaware—A Study in Attendance.* Bureau of Education Service Citizens of Delaware, University of Delaware Press, Newark, Del., 1925.

An analysis of the causes of nonattendance and some consequences of it. Advocates means for improving attendance. Shows that these means advanced attendance from an average of 86 days to an average of 133 days for all pupils enrolled.

CUBBERLEY, ELLWOOD P. *State and County Educational Reorganization.* Macmillan Company, 1918.

A revised school code for a hypothetical state. Discusses the school census, compulsory education, and child labor.

DAVIS, J. W. *First Annual Report of the Director of Attendance for the Year Ending July 31, 1915.* Department of Education of the City of New York, 1916.

Discusses the growth of compulsory education enforcement in New York City, the organization of the bureau of attendance, the work it has done, the effect of enforcement on attendance, prosecutions in court, and causes of truancy.

ELIOT, THOMAS D. *The Juvenile Court and the Community.* Macmillan Company, 1914.

Undertakes to show that the juvenile court is an unnecessary institution, and that the functions it performs should be performed by the school and the domestic relations court.

ELLWOOD, CHARLES A. "Our Compulsory Education Laws, and Retardation and Elimination in Our Public Schools." *Education,* May, 1914, p. 572.

Says our compulsory education laws are failures, because they are designed upon a wrong principle; namely, the principle of keeping the child in the school a definite length of time. Advocates a minimum education which should be required for every boy or girl.

EMMONS, FREDERICK E. *City School Attendance Service.* Teachers College, Columbia University, Contributions to Education, No. 200, 1926.

An intensive study of the organization and administration of the attendance service in fifteen selected cities. Sets up a practical program for the registration of the school population and for securing regularity of attendance.

ENSIGN, F. C. *Compulsory School Attendance and Child Labor.* Published by the author, Iowa City, Iowa, 1921.

Traces the growth of the idea of compulsory education from early English customs and laws through the colonial period and early national period. Then shows how legislation in regard to compulsory attendance at school and restriction of child labor developed in each of five selected states.

GIDEON, H. J. *Report of the Bureau of Compulsory Education for the Year Ending June 30, 1925.* Board of Public Education, Philadelphia.

A comprehensive survey of the work of an attendance bureau in a large city. Discusses attendance service, junior employment service, and the school census.

HANSON, WHITTIER L. *The Costs of Compulsory Attendance Service in the State of New York and Some Factors Affecting the Cost.* Bureau of Publications, Teachers College, Columbia University, Contributions to Education, No. 158, 1924.

The study is based on random samplings of the annual reports from the city and village superintendents, and the principals of union school districts in New York. Gives information on the organization of attendance departments, the degree to which the law is enforced, and the cost of enforcement.

HIATT, JAMES S. *The Truant Problem and the Parental School.* U. S. Bureau of Education, Bulletin, 1915, No. 29.

A study of 100 typical cases of truancy in Philadelphia. Involves the factors of nationality, age and sex, progress, retardation, mentality, causes, home surroundings. Studies also the parental schools in thirteen selected cities.

HICKS, F. C. *Materials and Methods of Legal Research.* The Lawyers' Coöperation Publishing Co., Rochester, N. Y., 1923.

Treats of the classes of law books and their use, of the materials and arrangements of books in law libraries, and contains an annotated bibliography of law books and articles about law books.

OPPENHEIMER, J. J. *The Visiting Teacher Movement.* Public Education Association of the City of New York, 1924.

A study of the history of the visiting teacher movement, the reasons for it, how it is organized and carried on, its relation to the attendance service, and its effect on improvement in scholarship.

REAVIS, GEORGE H. *Factors Controlling Attendance in Rural Schools.* Teachers College, Columbia University Contributions to Education, No. 108, 1920.

Fifty possible factors affecting rural school attendance in two hundred schools in Maryland are studied. Five of them found to be especially significant.

Report of the Committee Appointed by the Children's Bureau, August, 1921. "Juvenile Court Standards." U. S. Department of Labor, Children's Bureau Publication, No. 121, 1923.

A committee of fourteen child workers worked two years on the first draft of this report. The draft was submitted to two hundred persons interested in juvenile court work for criticism. The completed report was made May 18, 1923. It proposes fundamental principles for the organization and the procedures of juvenile courts.

Report of the Survey of Certain Aspects of the Public School System of Providence, R. I., 1923-24, pp. 54-65. Division of Field Studies, Institute of Educational Research, Teachers College, Columbia University, G. D. Strayer, Director.

Enumerates the adequate functions of an attendance department. Discuss the importance of courts in enforcing attendance.

Report of the Survey of the Public School System of Atlanta, Ga., 1921-22. Vol. II, pp. 40-60; 105-141. Division of Field Studies, Institute of Educational Research, Teachers College, Columbia University, G. D. Strayer, Director.

A description of the relationship of the schools to the courts in enforcing attendance.

Report of the Survey of the Public School System of Springfield, Mass, 1923-4, pp. 39-58. Division of Field Studies, Institute of Educational Research, Teachers College, Columbia University, G. D. Strayer, Director.

Describes the lax enforcement of the attendance law by the courts. Discusses the effect on parents and children.

Report of the Survey of the Schools of Watertown, N. Y., 1924-25, pp. 89-102. Division of Field Studies, Institute of Educational Research, Teachers College, Columbia University, G. D. Strayer, Director.

Gives the court record of the attendance officer for a number of years. Shows there was no serious effort by the court to enforce the law.

Ross, F. A. *School Attendance in 1920.* Government Printing Office, Washington, D. C., 1924.

A comprehensive analysis of school attendance in the United States from the data of the census of 1920. Shows what the attendance is by states, by urban and rural groups, and by race groups. Discusses the factors involved.

Shallow, Edward B. "Does a Strict Enforcement of the Compulsory Education Law Assist Teachers and Supervisors in Their Work?" *Proceedings of the National Education Association,* 1916, p. 1094.

Explains how a strict enforcement of the compulsory education law helps the work of teachers by increasing attendance, reducing retardation and conserving the teacher's nervous energy.

Snedden, David. "The Public School and Juvenile Delinquency." *Educational Review,* April, 1907, p. 374.

Discusses the function and value of the juvenile court in diagnosing the difficulties of juvenile delinquency.

Strayer, G. D., Engelhardt, N. L., et al. *Problems in Educational Administration.* Bureau of Publications, Teachers College, Columbia University, 1925.

Defines 116 practical problems in the various fields of educational administration. Provides data and suggestions for their solutions. Extensive bibliography for each problem.

The Survey. "Truancy in Milwaukee—The Work of a New Kind of Truant Officer." February 26, 1916, p. 637.

Describes the work of H. R. Pestalozzi in his endeavors as truant officer to understand and remove the causes of truancy, and to effect a closer coöperation between the home and classroom.